CHRIST AND THE KINGDOM

Christ and the Kingdom

A. M. Hunter

SERVANT BOOKS
Ann Arbor, Michigan

First American edition 1980 by:
Servant Books
P.O. Box 8617
Ann Arbor, Michigan 48107

First published 1980 by:
The Saint Andrew Press
121 George Street, Edinburgh EH2 4YN

Cover Illustration: Kevin Davidson
Cover Design: John B. Leidy

Printed in the United States of America
ISBN 0-89283-092-1

Contents

Preface

The substance of this book consists of lectures given in 1978 to an American (Methodist) School of Theology in Edinburgh University.

Scripture quotations are mostly from The Revised Standard Version or The New English Bible.

Once again I am deeply indebted to my friend, the Rev. David G. Gray, B.D., for valued help with the proof-reading

A. M. Hunter
Ayr
December 1979

Prologue

I

The Bible is the book of the people of God or, if dynamic terms be preferred, the book of the two Exoduses.

The Old Testament records God's call to Israel to be his people, that they in their turn might be 'a light to lighten the Gentiles'. It tells how he rescued them, through Moses, from Egyptian bondage, made a covenant with them at Sinai, and brought them, after long wandering, to the promised land. This was the First Exodus. It goes on to relate how down the centuries he disciplined them by blessing and judgment, speaking to them through 'his servants the prophets' and kindling in their hearts a hope of a time when he would crown his gracious dealings with them in the happiness of a new age.

The New Testament tells how God fulfilled his promises by inaugurating his saving rule in the work and words of Jesus. This is the Second Exodus (*Luke* 9:31; *1 Corinthians* 5:6-8, 10, 1-5). Sometimes we call this 'the Christ Event'. By this we mean all that Christ's coming involved, his historic ministry of course, but also his resurrection, the advent of the Holy Spirit, and the rise of the new Israel destined to become the holy catholic Church: 'the whole congregation of Christian people dispersed throughout the world'.

What is our warrant for reading the Bible thus? It is that of Christ himself. 'Think not', he said (*Matthew* 5:17), 'that I am come to destroy the law and the prophets' (i.e. the old revelation); 'I am not come to destroy but to fulfil them.' It is also apostolic. Paul said, 'All the promises of God' (i.e. those made to old Israel), 'find their Yes in him.' (*II Corinthians* 1:20).

Yet if Christ saw himself as heir to the messianic hope

of the prophets in old Israel, in living it out he crucified it, so that the crucified reality is better than all their foretellings. Jesus Christ, Christians believe, is a great divine dream come true, God's Amen to men.

II

The historical setting of the Christ Event may be briefly described. Matthew and Luke, taking us back to a Bethlehem cradle, tell of a boy born of a virgin through the special action of the Holy Spirit. It is their way of saying that God was uniquely there at work. Mark begins his account with a baptism administered by John, son of Zechariah, in the river Jordan during the reign of the Roman Emperor Tiberius.

Among the recipients of this baptism was a man known as Jesus of Nazareth but, locally, as 'the son of Mary' (*Mark* 6:3). Born in the reign of the Emperor Augustus, while the *Pax Romana* girdled the world, he had grown up in Nazareth of Galilee, accompanying his parents to the festivals in Jerusalem (*Luke* 2:41-51) and learning the trade of a carpenter. As a young man, he had shown uncommon skill in interpreting his people's scriptures, and from his later words and habits we may surmise that, though friendly to all men, he had a way of retiring into solitary places for prayer.

When the great Augustus died in AD 14, he must have been about twenty. Doubtless the news of the Emperor's death troubled many of his compatriots, fearful that it might mean the end of 'the Roman peace' and an ordered empire. But Jesus was thinking of another peace and another empire, and biding his God-appointed time. When a dozen or so years later the voice of prophecy, so long silent in Israel, rang out again in the Judean wilderness, Jesus knew that the time was near. He went down from

Nazareth to Jordan to be baptised by John—thus deliberately 'numbering himself with the transgressors' (*Isaiah* 53:12)—and, soon after, to begin a ministry in which he would proclaim a kingdom mightier than the Roman, a kingdom in which the king was no earthly potentate but an almighty heavenly Father.

III

What manner of man was this whose ministry was to change the course of history, so that to this very day we divide it into BC and AD?

Of Julius Caesar, whom some have accounted the greatest of men, Shakespeare makes one of his assassins say:

> His life was gentle, and the elements
> So mix'd in him that Nature might stand up
> And say to all the world, 'This was a man!'

Far more fitly might these words be applied to the Jesus of history. In him, as we read the gospels, we find a 'mixture', or rather a union of opposites, so that to limn his portrait we have to use paradox and antithesis:

Master of men and events, and come, like a Hebrew Prometheus, to set the earth aflame with the heavenly fire, he yet was a lover of little children and the champion of fallen women.

Stern critic of the Scribes' pedantry, a foe to all sham piety and hypocrisy, and one capable of driving at scourge-point the holy hucksters from the Temple, he yet was named 'the friend of publicans and sinners', and had a heart which went out in compassion to the shepherdless multitudes and to all the despised Zacchaeuses, Mary Magdalenes, and blind Bartimaeuses of this world.

Holding an almost sacramental view of the marriage

bond in the sphere of human relations he yet, in pursuance of his high calling, deliberately cut himself loose from all ties of family.

Convinced of Israel's divine vocation, he had an intense reverence for his people's past which yet was too small for him, so that 'it rent him to rend it' (*Luke* 19:41-44), as he had to, for the kingdom's sake.

'Gentle and lowly in heart', and 'taking the form of a servant'—the Servant of the Lord—he yet conjoined with his sublime humility a sovereign sense of authority, epitomised in his 'Amen I tell you', and the unshakeable conviction that he was ordained to play a unique part in God's judging and saving ways with men.

Matter-of-factness and mystery surround the Jesus of the gospels. On the one hand, we find the down-to-earthness, the feuds and factions, the hopes and despairs, of little Israel under Rome's dominion in the third decade of the first century; and the tale which the evangelists tell has its denouement in the wrenching of one man's flesh and the spilling of his blood, on a square of ground, outside the northern wall of Jerusalem, on an April morning in the year AD 30. On the other hand, we find the 'mystery'—what Otto called the *mysterium tremendum et fascinans*—that aura of a higher and holier world in which this Man lives and moves and has his being—so that in his presence, the Gospels tell us, men were 'amazed', 'astonished' and overcome by the holy terror men have felt in the presence of the uncanny, the supernatural.

Thus everywhere the gospel narrative is grounded in the soil of Palestine, and yet everywhere it sets us in the presence of the eternal.

So this story of stories, which still fascinates men the world over, goes on to tell how a humble Jewish maiden's son, proclaiming in 'Galilee of the Gentiles' the dawning of God's kingdom, eventually in Jerusalem, for sinners' sake, poured out his soul unto God and unto death and, 'being heard for his godly fear', as the writer to the Hebrews puts it, was raised by God from the grave to 'become the source of eternal salvation to all who obey him' (*Hebrews* 5:7ff).

In the second half of the first century, John summed up the story's meaning in a verse which Luther called 'the Gospel within the Gospels': 'God so loved the world that he gave his only Son that whoever believes in him should not perish but have eternal life.' (*John* 3:16).

Chapter 1

The Kingdom of the Father

I

In his classic study of the sayings of Jesus, T. W. Manson concluded that the cause for which Christ lived and died could best be summed up in one phrase 'the kingdom of my Father'.[1] Later we shall study what Christ taught about the fatherhood of God; but our first question must be, 'What does the kingdom of God mean?' No one disputes that it is the central theme of the gospels. With the news of God's dawning kingdom Jesus began his ministry; it is the burden, in one way or another, of all his parables; it is the theme on his lips at the Last Supper. In the thought of God's kingdom Jesus lives and works and dies.

But what does it signify? Modern men have returned many and various answers. 'The organisation of humanity through action inspired by love', says one. 'A spiritual commonwealth embracing all who do God's will', says another. The Bible's name for evolution, says a third. But perhaps the commonest view is that of some brave new social order to be built by men on Christian principles:

> Rise up, O men of God,
> His kingdom tarries long,
> Bring in the day of brotherhood
> And end the night of wrong.

All these answers are wide of the mark. The kingdom of God is not a matter of human organisation, or another name for the evolutionary process, or some Christian socialist's earthly paradise. In the gospels the kingdom is not man's deed but God's seed (*Mark* 4:26-29); not man striving but God acting. It is a power breaking into this world from the beyond, through the direct action of the living God. It is God in Christ invading history for us men and for our salvation.

The evidence for this you will find in any good modern commentary on the gospels. There you will be told that the phrase means the rule, or sovereignty, of God, and must be understood, not statically or territorially, but *dynamically*.[2] The basic idea is that of God acting on behalf of his people, to bring them the blessings of salvation. We may define it as God's sovereign activity in rescuing them from sin and evil and the new order of things thus inaugurated.

Now for the Jews the rule of God, so understood, was *the* great hope for the future. It was the End-event in which the whole long travail of history would find its meaning and God would complete his saving purpose for the world.[3]

With the news that this Event was now 'upon them' Christ opened his ministry. 'The time has come', he cried, 'the kingdom of God is upon you; repent and believe the Gospel' (*Mark* 1:15, *NEB*). The End-event, for which they had so often prayed, was at long last entering history. This is what our scholars call 'inaugurated eschatology', and for it there is ample evidence in the recorded words and works of Jesus.

Take, first, those sayings in which he declares that God's rule is a dawning reality. 'If I, by the finger of God, cast out devils, then is the kingdom of God come upon you' (*Luke* 11:20, Q); 'The law and the prophets were until John; since then the good news of the kingdom of God is preached' (*Luke* 16:16, Q); 'The Kingdom of God is in your midst' (*Luke* 17:21, *RSV*, *NEB*, *Jerusalem Bible*). To these we may add Jesus' words to his disciples: 'To you the secret of the kingdom of God has been given' (*Mark* 4:11), and 'Blessed are the eyes which see what you see! For I tell you, that many prophets and kings desired to see what you see, and did not see it, and to hear what you hear, and did not hear it.' (*Luke* 10:23f, Q).

To the same effect speaks parable after parable. The Sower, the Seed growing secretly, the Mustard Seed, the Leaven, the Drag-net, the Great Supper; all presuppose the rule, or reign, of God as a dawning reality. Note how they compare the kingdom not to some inert, static thing but to something in movement or to somebody doing something—yeast working among flour, a drag-net catching fish, a farmer sowing seed—so that each parable says in its different way: 'God is now active, in a new way, on behalf of his people. Now is the day of salvation.'

Lastly, consider the miracles of Jesus. What place had they in the good news he proclaimed? In one phrase, they were *the kingdom of God in action*, that is, tokens of the new era in which the power of God was at work through himself and his mission, meeting and defeating the devil and all his works, whether it was the demonic distortion of man's personality, or the assault of disease on his natural vigour, or the foretaste of death, 'the last enemy'. The 'mighty works' (*dunameis*) of Jesus were in fact the rule of God embodied in deeds of healing, outgoings in power to sick and sinful people of that love which was central to the kingdom of God. Signs of the presence of the kingdom, Jesus' miracles were, as he told the messengers from John the Baptist, fulfilments of the prophets' predictions concerning the messianic age. 'Are you the Coming One?' (i.e. the Messiah), John had asked from his prison. 'Go and tell John', said Jesus to his messengers, 'what you have seen and heard. The blind are receiving their sight, the lame walking, the lepers are being cleansed, the dead are being raised up, and the poor are having the good news preached to them.' (*Luke* 7:22, Q).[4]

Having discovered what the kingdom of God really means, the dawning of the blessed rule of God so long hoped and prayed for, we must now study five crucial corollaries, or correlatives, of the kingdom of God.

II

Corollary no 1 concerns the King in the kingdom. When Middleton Murry wrote in his *Life of Jesus*, 'the secret of the kingdom of God was that there was no King, only a Father', his paradox contained truth. *The King in Jesus' kingdom was a heavenly Father.* For proof we need look no further than the prayer he taught his disciples, 'Father . . . thy kingdom come!' (*Luke* 11:2), to which we may add another of his sayings to his chosen followers, 'Have no fear, little flock, your Father has chosen to give you the kingdom' (*Luke* 12:32 *NEB*).

Yet, contrary to what is often said, Jesus did not go about Galilee saying to the multitudes, 'God is your Father and you are all brothers.' The facts are these.[5] (1) Jesus himself addressed God as *Abba* (dear Father), using the Aramaic word Jewish children used at home in talking to their earthly fathers. Before Jesus no Jew had dared to apply this term of endearment to holy God. Jesus was the first to do so; and were there no other evidence, this fact alone would testify to his own sense of unique sonship to God. (2) In the earliest Gospel, *Mark*, Jesus speaks of God as Father only four times, and always to his disciples. God's fatherhood was therefore a *secret* which he disclosed to his disciples *in private*. And if we ask why, the answer is because the experience of God as Father was the deepest experience of his own spiritual life, not therefore something to be shouted from the housetops.

Men, he taught, may *become* sons of God; but for this supreme privilege they must become debtors to himself. 'No one comes to the Father except by me', he says in the fourth Gospel (*John* 14:6). Likewise, in his great thanksgiving Jesus says, 'No one knows the Father but the Son, and those to whom the Son may choose to reveal him' (*Matthew* 11:27, *NEB*).

Only after Pentecost, with the advent of the Holy Spirit, did Jesus' secret become an *open* secret, moving Paul, for example, to write to the Christians in Rome, 'The Spirit you have received is not a Spirit of slavery leading you back into a life of fear, but a Spirit that makes us sons, enabling us to cry "Abba! Father!"' (*Romans* 8:14f, *NEB*).

III

Corollary no 2: The Rule of God involves a new people of God, a Church. We sing:

> The Church's one foundation
> Is Jesus Christ her Lord,
> She is his new creation
> By water and the Word.

But in what sense is the Church 'Christ's creation'? As we have seen, Christ proclaimed that the rule of God was dawning. But what sort of king is he who has no subjects? What sort of sovereign who has no sphere of sovereignty? Nay, to use the language Christ himself preferred, what kind of heavenly Father who has no earthly family? In short, as convex always implies concave, so does the rule of God the Father imply a people living under his fatherly rule, a Church, a family of God.

Now let us take a second point. Prophets and psalmists

in old Israel had foretold that, when the Messiah came, his task would be to gather God's people (See *Ezekiel* 34:15f, 23f; *Micah* 5:6; *The Psalms of Solomon*,[6] 17). Pregnant as it was with political overtones, Jesus fought shy of using the title Messiah in public; but when he chose to call himself the Son of man, or likened himself to a shepherd and his disciples to a flock (*Luke* 12:32, 19:10; *John* 10:1-5 etc), he was making a veiled claim to be head of the new Israel, God's new people living under his Father's rule.

Call this, if you like, the theological theory of the matter. Now turn to the gospels and watch Jesus translating the theory into a living fact.

First: *Jesus called twelve men and taught them.* Note the number—it is that of the tribes in the old people of God. Clearly he is creating a new Israel and instructing it. In what? The answer is: in the ways of the dawning kingdom.

Second: *Jesus sent out the twelve as heralds of the kingdom.* (The mission, found in all synoptic sources, is one of the best attested facts in the life of Jesus.) What was the purpose of this mission? Let us recall that the rule of God is dynamic, it creates a people of God wherever its power is experienced. Jesus' aim, then, in sending out his missionaries was the ingathering of the new people of God.

Third: *when Jesus held the Last Supper, it was an act in the establishment of the Church.* 'This cup', he told his disciples, 'is the new covenant in my blood' (*I Corinthians* 11:25; *Mark* 14:24). A new covenant implies the establishment of a new people of God. On that fateful evening the twelve sat round the supper table as the nucleus of the new Israel, that community which sprang into effective life after the resurrection and the Day of Pentecost.

So, to those scholars who, not so long ago, told us that Jesus never intended to found a Church,[7] we may reply in the words with which Oliver Cromwell addressed the General Assembly of the Church of Scotland in 1650: 'I beseech you, in the bowels of Christ, think it possible you may be mistaken.'

IV

Corollary no 3: The Kingdom of God requires a new style of living. Our Lord's design for living in his Father's kingdom is best summarised in the Sermon on the Mount (*Matthew* 5-7) which is basically 'ripe teaching for ripe disciples'.[8] It is as if Jesus were saying to his men, 'Since the kingdom of God has dawned upon the world and you are living in it, you must begin to live in the kingdom way.'

Since we shall study the Sermon at some length in the next chapter, it will suffice here to make only two points:

First, the ethic (or moral teaching) of Jesus is not a new code of laws on the perfect keeping of which our salvation depends. If it were, we should all be doomed to damnation, since none of us measures up to the moral heights to which Christ calls us. Rather is it (as we shall see) *an ethic of grace*, man's grateful response in living to the grace of God who brings in his kingdom.

Second, the most distinctive element in the new style of life prescribed by Jesus is the commandment of love (*agapé*), for Jesus interprets the whole duty of man to his fellow-man in terms of the verb 'to love'. But, by 'love' he does not mean anything sentimental or erotic, neither does he mean that we must resolve to 'like' other people.[9] By 'loving' he means 'caring'—caring practically and selflessly, as the Good Samaritan did, for all who meet us on life's road, caring not merely for the decent and the deserving but for all who need our help, even enemies.

This is the new 'law' of the kingdom because the King in the kingdom is an almighty Father who himself cares for the ungracious and the ungrateful.

V

Corollary no 4: The kingdom is centred in Christ. 'If *I* by the finger of God cast out devils', said Jesus, 'then is the kingdom of God come upon you' (*Luke* 11:20, Q). Here speaks One who incarnates the kingdom. Elsewhere to follow Jesus is to be *in* the kingdom. Where he is, the kingdom is. Somehow in the gospels the kingdom *is* Christ himself.[10]

Why is this not clearer in the gospel record? Because Jesus refused to call himself the Messiah in public, knowing that that title was fatally loaded with political connotations. Instead, he chose the cryptic title of the Son of man, cryptic because it could mean simply 'man', or it could denote a mysterious messianic figure, 'the Man'.

For a clue to this go back to the famous vision in *Daniel* 7. First, we read of the rise and fall of four beasts symbolising the despotic heads of four world empires. (Don't we still today talk of 'the British Lion' and 'the Russian Bear'?) Then there appears one 'like a son of man' who is exalted in order to receive from God a universal and eternal kingdom. Finally, we learn that 'the saints of the Most High', i.e. the people of God, receive and possess the kingdom for ever.

'Son of man . . . a kingdom . . . the saints of the Most High.' Translate the vision into Galilean terms, and it will read: 'God gives the kingdom to Jesus the Son of man who mediates it to his disciples as the new people of God.'

In Daniel's vision the Son of man, though human, is a figure with a heavenly destiny. In the Gospels, however, he is one who must suffer and die if there is to be any sovereignty for him and his. Why so? Because God has willed that the Son of man must tread the path marked out for the servant of the Lord (*Isaiah* 53. Cf *Mark* 10:45).

One more thing, and that of capital importance, falls to be said. Think of God's new order as a kingdom, and its Bearer may well call himself the Son of man. But, if the King in the kingdom is a Father, then only one word will describe him who brings it to men, the word 'Son'. And this is why Jesus speaks of God as 'my Father' and calls himself God's Son, or 'the Son' (*Matthew* 16:17, *Mark* 1:11, 12:1-9, 13:32, *Matthew* 11:27 etc). A filial relation to the divine Father, unparalleled in history, is the last and deepest secret of the Jesus of the gospels.

VI

Corollary no 5: The kingdom involves a cross. Jesus is both the herald of the kingdom (*Mark* 1:15) and the Son of man who must suffer and die (*Mark* 10:45). Thus he poses in his own person the problem of the kingdom and the cross.

Since the kingdom was initiated in his ministry, we may not say (as some have said[11]) that he died to bring it in. The cross must fall *within* the kingdom, form its burning focus and climax, the end which crowns his earthly work.

One who read his God-appointed destiny in terms of Isaiah's Servant of the Lord must from the outset have reckoned with the possibility of a cross. When at Caesarea Philippi he told his disciples what messiahship meant for him, there was 'death in the cup' his Father had given him to drink (*Mark* 8:31). But, by the same token, if death awaited him, by it, as men would live to see, the kingdom of God would come 'with power' (*Mark* 9:1). It is the very phrase the early Christians used of Christ's resurrection: 'appointed Son of God with power' (*Romans*

1:4). The cross, then, was the condition not of the kingdom's coming but of its coming with power, its effectuation.

Nor is this unsupported speculation. It is confirmed by another saying of Jesus—genuine if any saying of his deserves this description—about the 'fire' he came to kindle on earth and the 'baptism' of blood he must undergo if the fire were to be lit. 'I have come to set fire to the earth, and how I wish it were already kindled! I have a baptism to undergo, and what constraint I am under until the ordeal is over!' (*Luke* 12:49f, Q, *NEB*). The *Te Deum* is right. It was when Jesus 'had overcome the sharpness of death' that he 'opened the kingdom of heaven to all believers.'

VII

We have covered so much ground that we had better here recapitulate our findings. The kingdom of God means God invading history for men's salvation. In this kingdom the King is a Father, as his rule implies both a new people of God and a new life-style. Centred in Christ, it requires for its effectuation a cross.

One important matter, the consummation of the kingdom, we shall discuss in a later chapter on the Last Things. But, to round off this one, we may briefly touch on some of the things then to be said.

What did Jesus teach about the *future* kingdom? Some of his sayings about it refer to the heavenly world where God's rule does not come or go but is eternally present. Thus, 'many will come from east and west and sit at table with Abraham, Isaac and Jacob in the kingdom of heaven' (*Matthew* 8:11, Q). Other sayings, however, imply a coming of the kingdom, or the Son of man—for the two are not to be separated—*in history*. Thus he prophesies that after a very short time the Son of man will rise from the dead (*Mark* 8:31) or, standing on trial before Caiaphas (*Mark* 14:62), he declares that the Son of man will 'be seen sitting at God's right hand and coming with the clouds of heaven', a prediction of his exaltation to the presence of God.[12] Apparent defeat, he tells his judge, will be followed by swift vindication for himself and his cause. What happened we know: Christ's Easter victory, the coming of the promised Spirit, the rise of the early Church. This was Christ's coming *in* history.

But there was also to be another one *beyond* history. Thus in his parable about the last judgment (*Matthew* 25:31-46) he sets the 'glorious' coming of the Son of man in another world than this one, for it is not in this world of space and time that all the nations, dead as well as living, will appear before him. This is the consummation of the kingdom of God. What will it mean?

First, the 'finalising' of the work God took in hand when he sent Christ into the world (*I Corinthians* 15:24-28).

Second, the confrontation of all mankind by God in Christ. This is what is meant by his second coming, and our clue to it is his first coming. God has already revealed himself in a Man from whom we may learn with what sort of person we shall have to do when our race reaches its last frontier post:

> Then will he come with meekness for his glory,
>> God in a workman's jacket as before,
> Living again the eternal Gospel story,
>> Sweeping the shavings from his workshop floor.[13]

But if this final coming will involve judgment, as our Lord says it will, equally it will mean the perfect fruition of life in the eternal kingdom of God. Then the promises of the beatitudes will come fully true: the mourners will be comforted, the merciful will obtain mercy, the pure in heart will see God, and Christ's faithful followers will be for ever at home in what he called his Father's house (*John* 14:2).

When will the consummation of the kingdom take place? We do not know, neither did the incarnate Son of God himself (*Mark* 13:32). It is a reserved secret in the breast of God.

Nor is it the Christian's business to speculate on 'the day or the hour'. It has been well said that New Testament thought about the Last Things, at its deepest and best, always concentrates on what God has already done for men in his gift to us of Christ. It does not ask, 'How long will it be before the final whistle blows "full time"?' Rather it asks, 'Where ought I to be to receive the next pass?' What really matters is that the kick-off has already taken place, the game is on, and we have a Captain to lead us to victory.[14]

NOTES

1. *The Sayings of Jesus*, p 345.

2. 'The kingdom of Heaven', the phrase preferred by Matthew, means the same thing; the words 'of Heaven' merely illustrating the pious Jew's avoidance of the divine name. Compare our use of the word 'Providence' when we mean God.

3. For the evidence see C. H. Dodd, *Parables of the Kingdom*, pp 34ff.

4. Jesus couches his reply in words echoing the great promises of Isaiah (*Isaiah* 26:19, 29:18f, 35:5f, 61:1).

5. See T. W. Manson, *The Teaching of Jesus*, chapter 4. In the gospels Jesus very rarely uses the verb 'to rule' with God as subject, or speaks of God as King.

6. A collection of psalms, written probably about 50 BC by a Pharisee, and to be found in *The Apocrypha and Pseudepigrapha of the Old Testament*, ii, pp 625-652.

7. e.g. Jackson and Lake, *The Beginnings of Christianity*, vol I, p 317.

8. C. G. Montefiore, *The Synoptic Gospels*, II, p 27.

9. Christians of course should make an effort to control their emotional dislike.

10. Origen, in the third century, coined the phrase *autobasileia*: 'himself the kingdom'.

11. e.g. R. H. Fuller in *The Mission and Achievement of Jesus*, chapter 3.

12. This interpretation of *Mark* 14:62 is now generally accepted by scholars. The reference is to Christ's 'enthronement'. See V. Taylor, *Mark*, p 569.

13. G. A. Studdert-Kennedy (better known as 'Woodbine Willie').

14. C. F. D. Moule, *The Birth of the New Testament*, p 101.

Chapter 2

The Way of the Kingdom
(*Matthew* 5-7)

The early Christians were known as 'men and women who followed the Way' (*Acts* 9:2 etc), the word 'Way' referring to their distinctive lifestyle. 'See how these Christians love one another', their pagan neighbours are reported to have said. What 'Way' was this? It was the way of life Christ had taught his disciples in what is known as the Sermon on the Mount, by many accounted the supreme utterance on the good life.

Yet how variously men have interpreted it! For Tolstoy, it was a new law, to be taken quite literally and applied universally.[1] For Albert Schweitzer, it was 'an interim ethic', an emergency code of ethics for the brief interval between Christ's ministry, and a cataclysmic end of the world which never came.[2]

On the other hand, when the popular press today turns 'religious', it supposes the Sermon to be all 'plain sailing'—straightforward rules for living which, if they could be written into the statute-books of the nations and implemented, would usher in heaven upon earth.

But is the Sermon indeed all 'plain sailing'? Is it a morality for all men? To whom was it originally delivered? Did Jesus intend it to be a new law as binding on his new Israel, the Church, as the Law of Moses was on old Israel? And what guidance on the good life can the Sermon give us today who live in other times, under other skies, and are vexed by problems unknown to the first

Christians? These are some of the questions to which we must find answers.

I

But, first, to the *making* of the Sermon.

The Sermon (of which we have a shorter version in *Luke* 6:20-49) is the first of five great discourses in Matthew's gospel. He introduces it thus:

'When Jesus saw the crowds, he went up the hill [or 'into the hill country']. There he took his seat, and when his disciples had gathered round him, he began to address them' (*Matthew* 5:1f *NEB*).

The ordinary man or woman, hearing these words read in church, naturally concludes that Jesus uttered the following one hundred and seven verses in a single non-stop discourse, and possibly supposes that his disciple Matthew, like some modern reporter, made notes of it which, later, he incorporated in his gospel.

The truth is not so simple. We need not doubt that Jesus gave this teaching to his men in some such solitary setting, but we may be sure that he did not give them it all at one single session. Had he done so, only disciples with phenomenal memories would have remembered it all, as they would certainly have suffered from spiritual indigestion! Rather, the Sermon gathers into one splendid whole the teachings which Jesus gave his disciples on many occasions when he was training them to be 'apprentices' in the work of the kingdom.

How it all began, a knowledge of Jewish teaching methods will make clear. First, the teacher would talk to his disciples on some chosen topic: then he would sum everything up in a few pointed sentences; finally, he would go over these with his hearers till they had them by heart. Modern educationists may dismiss this as 'parrot learning', but there is more wisdom in the method than they allow. This must have been our Lord's way. But, by the evidence of the gospels, he did more than this. It is common knowledge that verse is much easier to memorise than prose. We need think only of our rhyme for remembering the months of the year: 'Thirty days hath September, April, June and November . . . etc'. Now a study[3] of the Sermon's style shows that Christ cast much of his teaching in poetic couplets and stanzas, so that it might stick in his hearers' memories. For example, on the subject of prayer:

> Ask, and it will be given you,
> Seek, and you will find,
> Knock, and it will be opened to you.

> For every one who asks receives,
> And he who seeks finds,
> And to him who knocks it will be opened (*Matthew* 7:7f).

Here we have two stanzas, each with three lines, which can be memorised without much difficulty.

Such were the beginnings of the Sermon. So, in quiet teaching-sessions, Jesus gave his disciples a pattern for living as God meant them to live in his kingdom. How all this teaching came to be set down in writing and collected into the masterly compendium we now have, is a complicated story, involving discussion of gospel sources, with which we need not now trouble ourselves.[4]

Enough to say that the present shape of the Sermon suggests that Matthew had in mind the needs of new converts when he put Christ's teaching down on paper. Jesus had shown the first entrants into the kingdom how God meant them to live. What more natural than that, after the resurrection and the coming of the Spirit, apostles and church teachers, wishing to set before their converts the moral ideal to which they were called, should have gathered Christ's teachings as Matthew has done, to be a design for living in God's new order.

II

Now let us study the *matter* of the Sermon. There are seven main themes:

1. *The people God calls divinely happy* (5:3-16)

In other words, the beatitudes. 'Recipes for happiness', somebody has called them; but they are not conventional ones. For Jesus turns the world's notions of happiness upside down, congratulating those whom the world despises. 'Blessed are the poor in spirit', he begins. By this he does not mean the poor-spirited but (as the *NEB* has it) 'those who know their need of God'. When he calls the mourners blessed, he has primarily in mind those who mourn the eclipse of God's cause in the world.[5] 'How blest are those of a gentle spirit', he says, and proceeds to call divinely happy the hungerers after righteousness, the compassionate, the pure in heart (i.e. the single-minded, the sincere) and the peace-makers. He ends by pronouncing 'blessed' those persecuted in the cause of right.

Gladness in hardship is therefore a main motif in the beatitudes; but those who show it are promised a heavenly reward. They shall be comforted, obtain mercy, see God, and so on; the future tenses emphasising certainty and not simply futurity.

There follow two little parables indicating the influence for good his disciples are to be among their fellow-men. 'You are to be the *salt* of the earth', he says (i.e. God's means for preserving the world from decay). And 'you are to be *light*'—to illuminate its darkness.

2. *The goodness God demands* (5:17-48)

Here we have a six-fold refrain: 'You have heard it was said to the men of old, but *I* say unto you'. Over against the dictates of the old law, Jesus sets God's new design for conduct in his kingdom.

Freud has dwelt much on 'depth-psychology'. What Christ calls for in his six antitheses is 'depth-morality'. Thus, to take only two examples: The old law said, 'You shall not commit adultery'; I say, 'No lust!' Again, the old law said, 'You shall not commit murder'; I say, 'No anger!' What God demands is *heart*-righteousness—the 'heart' being, in the Bible, and for Jesus, the seat and centre of the moral life. (Compare Robert Burns's 'The heart aye's the part aye that makes us right or wrang.'). And this section on the new goodness of the kingdom ends with Jesus calling his disciples to be as 'perfect' in their love for men, as God himself is.

3. *The piety God rewards* (6:1-18)

Now Jesus turns from a disciple's moral righteousness to his religious righteousness; namely, charity, prayer and fasting.

Whatever form your piety takes, he says, the one thing which matters is sincerity before God, as the one thing God condemns is a piety which 'sounds a trumpet' before it, i.e. which aims at buying the applause of men. This is hypocrisy: play-acting. Such men's piety is really a commercial transaction. What they are after are the plaudits of men. They get them there and then, and that is all the reward they are ever going to get. The account is closed. Therefore never publicise your piety. The secret of religion is religion in secret; this alone is sure of a divine reward.

4. *The service God requires* (6:19-24)

From piety, Jesus turns to the subject of earthly possessions. 'Lay not up for yourselves treasures upon the earth', he says. What he here forbids is the selfish accumulation of 'perishable goods'. The only treasures exempt from the ravages of time and beyond the reach of thieves are the heavenly ones—not what the world calls 'gilt-edged securities', but golden deeds of kindness and of love. Therefore, he says, with single-minded devotion set your hearts on these. No man can divide his allegiance between God and mammon. For where his treasure is, there will his heart be also.

5. *The faith to which God summons* (6:25-34)

Food, drink, and clothes—how we mortals allow the quest for such commodities to absorb our waking thoughts! 'But', says Jesus, 'to be constantly worrying about them is to miss the true end of life. The secret of serenity, as you may learn from the wild birds or the lilies, is reliance on a heavenly Father able to supply his children's wants. Your concern should be for his kingdom and his righteousness. All else leave in his wise hands. It is folly to add tomorrow's worries to today's.'

6. *The way to treat others* (7:1-12)

'Beware of judging your brother—you may be a much bigger sinner than he is! If you are not ready to show mercy to him, how can you expect mercy from the Judge of all?'

Again, don't press the pearl of the gospel on men who despise it. And keep on praying. If earthly fathers, sinful as they are, know how to give good gifts to their children, how much more does your heavenly Father! The golden rule is to do to others as you would have them do to you.' (That is, put yourself in the other man's place, and ask yourself, 'How would I like to be treated in that situation?')

7. *Profession and practice* (7:13-27)

Finally, in the little parables of the Two Ways (one of life, the other of death), the Two Trees (one producing good fruit, the other bad) and the Two Houses (one built on rock, the other on sand) Jesus challenges his disciples to build their lives on the divine pattern he has given them. In the closing parable he says, 'Either you act my way, which is God's way, or you court disaster, like the man who built his house on shifting sand.'

The Sermon raises three main questions. One, what is its place in the gospel? Two, was it meant for disciples or for all men? Three, is it a new law superseding the Law of Moses?

Before we attempt answers, one point—often forgotten—must be made. We shall not understand the Sermon until we set it against the background of the gospel Jesus preached: 'The kingdom of God is upon you' (*Mark* 1:15). The burden of all his work and words was his proclamation that God's gracious rule had dawned.[6] This is the grand presupposition of everything in the Sermon. It sketches the way of life for all who, by repentance and faith, have accepted the good news of God's forgiving grace which his rule brings with it.

If then Jesus says, 'You must forgive others', it is because they have already been assured, 'Your sins are forgiven'. If he bids his hearers live as 'sons of God' it is because, through him, they are already God's adopted sons. If he commands them to 'love their enemies', behind the command lies the dynamic of the boundless grace of God who sends his sun and rain on good and bad men alike. It is a matter of 'Freely you have received, therefore freely give' (*Matthew* 10:8). In short, the ethic of the Sermon is an *ethic of grace* (as indeed the whole New Testament ethic is). John sums it up in seven words: 'We love, because he first loved us' (*I John* 4:19). 'In the New Testament', said Thomas Erskine, 'religion is grace, and ethics is gratitude.'

Now we may answer our three questions:

First, the Sermon is *not* the gospel, but the way of life which ought to flow from it. The gospel tells of something God has *done*, that in Christ he has come into the world to save it. But this message of the grace of God carries with it a consequence for conduct. All those who, by following Christ, are 'in the kingdom' must live in the kingdom way. This way the Sermon outlines.

From this follows the answer to our second question. The Sermon is essentially disciple-teaching. It was intended not for all and sundry but for *committed* men, men who had confessed Christ as Master and Lord.

The third question is, 'Did Jesus intend the Sermon to be a new law of Moses on the perfect keeping of which men's salvation would depend?' The answer is 'No'. If this had been so, then Jesus who invited all weighed down by the old law's burdens to 'come to him', to 'take his yoke upon them', and to 'find rest' (*Matthew* 11:28f), would have been laying on his followers far heavier loads than ever he accused the Scribes and Pharisees of laying upon theirs (see *Matthew* 23:4). This is incredible. Jesus was no such legislator. What he gave his disciples in the Sermon was *principles of action* to govern their lives in God's new order of grace. The Sermon is not a new code of laws but a design for living. It is a compass, not an ordnance map. It provides direction, not directions.

III

Our final task is to consider the Sermon's relevance for Christians today. In other words, is the 'direction' which it supplies meant for actual living, or is it a counsel of perfection? We believe that the right answer is: both. 'You can receive a sacrament and you can find salvation', says a character in one of Rose Macaulay's novels, 'but you can't live the Sermon on the Mount.' This certainly was not the view of Christ, as witness the story of the Two Builders which closes the Sermon. Listen to him, 'Whoever hears these words of mine and *acts upon* them . . . ' (*Matthew* 7:24 *NEB*).

Yet still today many hold that 'you can't live the Sermon on the Mount'. They dismiss Christ's teaching as impossibly idealistic and, as proof, instance what he says about 'turning the other cheek' and 'loving your enemies'. What, they demand, would have happened to us in 1939 if we had turned the other cheek to Hitler and tried to love his Nazis?

To such people the answer is that this question does not arise in the passage they refer to (*Matthew* 5:38-42). Here Jesus is talking to his disciples about personal relations; and what he says is not (as the *AV* has it) 'resist not evil', but 'Do not set yourself against the man who wrongs you' (*NEB*). What Christ enunciates here is the principle of 'overcoming evil with good' (*Romans* 12:21) when you have a quarrel with another man. And Jesus proceeds to drive his point home with four mini-illustrations: The first is an assault; the second, a suit at law; the third, an official demand; and the fourth, a request for help.

The phrase about 'turning the other cheek' has hidden humour in it. 'If a man hits you on the right cheek', Jesus said (a pause while each disciple thought furiously about what was to be done, and then Jesus' completion of his sentence must have taken all their breaths away). 'Well', he said, 'you have another one, haven't you?'

As for the second illustration, a man who gave his legal opponent both his 'shirt' and his 'coat' would leave himself in a state of nudity—conclusive proof that Christ's saying was meant to illustrate a principle, and is not to be construed with unimaginative literalism.

In the third illustration we are to imagine a Roman soldier 'commandeering' a nearby Jew with, 'Here, shoulder this bag of mine, and get moving!' When this happens, and you have done the mile he demands, says Jesus, then disarm him by carrying his bag a further mile. The principle here is that of countering harshness with kindness.

'Give to him who asks you', the fourth mini-illustration, sounds like a command to indiscriminate charity, and most of us know to what evils this can lead. (The saintly William Law gave away two thousand five hundred pounds each year to beggars in his backyard, and succeeded in demoralising the neighbourhood!) Once again, it is the principle that matters, namely, that of generous reaction to genuine human need.

Take these sayings of Jesus, therefore, with a wooden literalism, and you miss their real meaning. Literal obedience to them (such as Tolstoy enjoined) would merely result in violence, robbery and anarchy.

Even so, it may be asked, does Christ's teaching work in actual practice? Of course it does. There are numberless cases and situations where Christ's principle does justify itself in practice, and good people carry it out. To stifle an angry reaction to a personal insult, to go the second mile, to be open-handed to the needy, is not this the kingdom way, and do not such actions wonderfully sweeten human relations in a hard and often selfish world?

Now consider Christ's command about loving enemies (*Matthew* 5:43-48). This is the crown of his love-ethic. Elsewhere (*Mark* 12:28f) he puts love of neighbour

second only to love of God. In his story about the Good
Samaritan (*Luke* 10:25-37) he refuses to set limits to the
scope of the word 'neighbour'. Here in the Sermon, he
carries matters to their spiritually-logical conclusion, love
for a persecuting enemy.

Does this mean that Christians should love organisa-
tions like the IRA Provisionals who inflict suffering and
death on innocent people? No, indeed. Once again, it is
not attitudes to enemies of the state but personal relations
that are in view.

Moreover, loving is not the same thing as liking. As
Jesus who 'knew what was in man' (*John* 2:25) was well
aware, there are people whom we do not naturally 'like'.
How, for instance, can we 'like' people who break up our
marriage or lead our children into evil ways? When Jesus
bids us love our enemies, he does not mean that we are to
love them as we do our wives or families. No, but he does
mean that we are to 'copy God' who sends his rain and
sun on good and bad alike. Whether we 'like' certain
people or not, we are to care for them, to treat them with
persistent and practical goodwill, simply because such
caring is God's way. Such caring, even for the unlovely
and the unlovable, is the very essence of Christian love, or
agapé.

Christ's teaching about 'turning the other cheek' and
loving enemies, thus understood, is not so 'impossible' as
people think. Yet, if some still maintain that such teaching
is 'beyond them', let us remember that he who called his
disciples to practise it, also described it as 'a counsel of
perfection'. 'You must be perfect', he said, 'as your
heavenly Father is perfect' (*Matthew* 5:48).

In other words, our Lord holds out before his followers
the challenge of the ideal. And is not this what any true
Christian ethic should still do today? Robert Browning

surely took this point when he wrote in *Andrea Del Sarto*:

A man's reach should exceed his grasp.
Or what's a heaven for?

None of us, this side of eternity, ever measures up to the standards of the Sermon. If we judge ourselves by them, we stand convicted as sinners who come short of the glory of God. Yet, if no man ever attains the heights set before us in the Sermon, this but illustrates the tension between the ideal and the actual which must always, in this fallen world, be our portion. For we, who are 'citizens of a commonwealth which is in heaven' (*Philippians* 3:20), have to live out our lives in a world where evil and temptation beset us at every turn. Nevertheless, though the ideal held up before us in the Sermon must ever 'exceed our grasp', we are yet called on, day by day, to keep aiming at it.

Nor are we left to do it alone, for he who gave us the Sermon is not just the past embodiment in a human life of perfect goodness. By the miracle of the resurrection he is a living and reigning Lord who still, through the Holy Spirit, comes to his people today, 'unseen but not unknown'. For all prepared to follow, this Christ is here to lead the way. Not only so, but in union with him lies also the strength to follow, as countless Christians from Paul onwards have testified. As T W Manson put it, 'The living Christ still has two hands, one to point the way, and the other held out to help us along.'[7]

So the Christian ideal set before us in the Sermon is not an ethical Everest to be scaled by our own sweat and striving. It is rather a road on which we may walk upwards with the living Christ as guide and friend. More, we have his own word that he will be with us to the end of the road. For does he not still promise us as he promised his first followers after he was risen from the dead, 'Lo, I am with you alway, even unto the end of the world'?

One closing practical suggestion. Today we are living in a society whose hedonistic materialism, greed and permissiveness have driven many idealists into open revolt against it. Moreover, though the Christian Church ought to be providing a moral guide to society, too often it conforms to the world around when, by the teaching of Christ and his apostles, it ought to be *different*. (Cf *Matthew* 6:7, 'Be not like them' and *Romans* 12:2, 'Do not be conformed to this world', i.e. 'Don't try to be "with it".')

What the Church ought to be launching is a Christian counter-attack against the evils in our society. But where are we to find a blue-print for such an offensive? Why not in the Sermon on the Mount? Here, ready to hand, is a moral manifesto, a summary of Christian principles and ideals which all who long for a moral and spiritual renaissance might use to show the sort of society properly deserving the name of Christian.[8]

NOTES

1. For Tolstoy, Christ's 'Judge not that you be not judged' meant 'Pull down your law-courts', and 'Resist not evil' meant 'Scrap your police forces'—sure recipes for lawlessness, mob rule and anarchy.
2. Schweitzer got the eschatology of the gospels wrong (as Otto, Dodd and others have shown) turning a Nelsonian eye on all those sayings and parables of Jesus which speak of God's kingdom as a dawning and blessed reality.
3. See C. F. Burney's *The Poetry of our Lord*.
4. See the author's *Design for Life*, pp 11-17.
5. People like Simeon who 'looked forward to Israel's comforting' (*paraklēsis*) *Luke* 2:25.

6. 'Every such precept depends upon a major premise, "The Kingdom of God has come upon you".' C. H. Dodd, *The Bible for Today*, p 83.
7. *Ethics and the Gospel*, p 68.
8. Such an exposition is to be found in J. R. W. Stott's *Christian Counter-culture* (Inter-varsity Press, 1978). See also Dietrich Bonhoeffer's *The Cost of Discipleship* (SCM Press, 1948).

Chapter 3

The Parables of the Kingdom

I

When the little girl was asked which bits of the Bible pleased her best, she replied: 'The like sayings'. She meant those stories in the gospels which often begin, 'The kingdom of God is like . . .', i.e. the parables. There are no more famous short stories in the world, as we quote them unconsciously every day. We talk about 'acting the Good Samaritan' or 'passing by on the other side'. Some of us use our 'talents' rightly; others 'hide their lamp under a bushel'; and others again indulge in 'riotous living'. We 'count the cost', or we leave things to 'the eleventh hour', and so on.

What many Christians do not realise is that we may now understand the parables better than our fathers and forefathers ever did.

For centuries the universal practice was to treat them as allegories (like *The Pilgrim's Progress*), i.e. as stories in which every detail had to be decoded and given a spiritual meaning. More recently, the fashion has been to *moralise* them, that is to say, make them to teach obvious moral truisms. Now, in this century, thanks principally to two great scholars, C. H. Dodd and Joachim Jeremias, our understanding of the parables has been revolutionised.

But let us begin at the beginning.

In the gospels we have more than sixty of Jesus' parables, and nowhere can we be surer that we are in direct touch with 'the mind of Christ' than in these vivid stories. And this for three reasons:

One, because the parables reflect daily life in first-century Palestine[1] as surely as the poems of Burns reflect that of Ayrshire in eighteenth-century Scotland.

Two, because 'the style is the man', i.e. the parables reveal our Lord's highly original way of thinking and speaking, his invincible faith in God his Father, the swift surprises of thought which were so characteristic of him, his telling use of hyperbole in order to drive a point home.[2]

And, three, because great parables are so difficult to create that it is hard to name another person in history with more than one or two to his credit.

But here let us sound a warning. It is wrong to regard his parables merely as picturesque stories from which we may draw edifying morals today. Here is a statement well worth pondering: 'Jesus told parables, and Jesus was put to death'.[3] Would men ever have crucified Jesus if he had simply gone about telling pleasant moralising tales? Of course they wouldn't! The truth is that many of Jesus' parables were more like Churchill's speeches in 1940, 'weapons of war' in a great campaign, the kingdom of God against the powers of evil.

Next, remember that Jesus' parables are parables of the kingdom and are all connected, directly or indirectly, with the good news he came proclaiming—the dawning of the rule of God in which the King in the kingdom was a holy heavenly Father. For the kingdom in the gospels is God's work, not man's. It is not some kind of Christian Utopia to be built by men, like William Blake's Jerusalem, 'in England's green and pleasant land'. It is divine power, from the unseen world, breaking into this one, in order to save. And Jesus' 'good news' was that this rule of God, for which men had long hoped and prayed, was now invading history in his own mission and message.

'Earthly stories with heavenly meanings' some of us

were taught in Sunday School to define the parables. It would be more accurate to call them 'earthly stories with kingdom of God meanings'.

The parables fall, roughly, into four classes:

(1) Some like the Sower, the Seed growing secretly, the Mustard Seed and the Leaven tell of the coming and growth of God's rule.

(2) Others like the Lost Sheep, the Prodigal Son (better, the Gracious Father) and the Labourers in the Vineyard (better, the Good Employer) proclaim the grace of the God now inaugurating his rule, and take us to the very heart of Jesus' good news.

(3) Others, again, like the Hidden Treasure, the Costly Pearl and the Two Builders, suggest the kind of men required for entry into the kingdom.

(4) Some, heavy with a sense of the impending doom over Israel, suggest the fateful crisis of Jesus' Jerusalem ministry. These include the Weather Signs (*Luke* 12:54ff); the Way to Court (*Luke* 12:57ff); the Shut Door (*Luke* 13:23ff); the Traveller at Sunset (*John* 12:35f); and the Wicked Tenants (or the Owner's Son, *Mark* 12:1-9).

Besides these, one or two parables like Dives and Lazarus (better, Rich Man, Poor Man) and the Sheep and the Goats look away to the time when God will consummate his kingdom in the last judgment and the glories of another and better world.

II

Now let us pick out five points to remember if we are to interpret the parables aright.

Point 1: Jesus' parables are not fables or fairy tales like Aesop's or Hans Andersen's, they are *stories from real life*. They are stories about baking and building, farming and fishing, weddings and funerals; stories about rich men and poor men, improvident bridesmaids and warring kings, importunate widows and rascally business men, 'Holy Willies' and ne'er-do-well sons.

Point 2: Jesus used parables not simply because 'truth embodied in a tale' sticks in the memory but because, by its very nature, the parable *teases into thought and calls for a decision*. Thus, when he ends a parable with the statement 'He who has ears to hear, let him hear!' he means, 'This is more than just a pleasant story. Go and work out its meaning for yourselves, and when you have found it, act!'

Point 3: As a rule, *a parable makes one point only*, and the descriptive details in the story are like the feathers which wing the arrow to its mark. This means that we are not to seek for deep hidden meanings in the details, like the 'two pence' in the Good Samaritan or 'the fatted calf' in the Prodigal Son.

Point 4: The parables *form a running commentary on Jesus' ministry*, first in Galilee and then in Jerusalem, and serve as prelude to the act which crowned and completed his earthly work, the cross (*John* 19:30). For there came a time when words were no longer of any avail, when only a deed could effect what God had sent Christ into the world to do.

The cross was in fact *God's* great parable acted out in the stuff of history, whereby he reconciled a prodigal human race to himself. Paul took the point. 'God was in Christ', he wrote, 'reconciling the world to himself' (*2 Corinthians* 5:19); and again: 'God shows his love for us in that, while we were yet sinners, Christ died for us.' (*Romans* 5:8).

Point 5: The parables of Jesus, like *all great works of art,*[4] *are perennial*, as he who told them is 'the same yesterday, today and for ever' (*Hebrews* 13:8). His

parables have a way of breaking the shackles of time and
speaking the Word of God to every age. (This is really the
work of the Holy Spirit, 'taking', as John put it, 'of the
things of Christ and showing them to us'. *John* 16:14.)

So, stories told long ago in Galilee and Jerusalem
continue to speak God's truth to us in the twentieth
century. They assure us that, as the hymn puts it, 'God's
kingdom stands and grows for ever'; they proclaim God's
forgiving grace for penitent sinners; they tell us what kind
of people God needs to do his work in the world today;
and they confront us with the eternal issues which hang
upon our decisions when faced with God's challenge to us
in Christ.

III

Now, by a few examples, let us see how the parables may
be interpreted so as to speak their truth to us.

But first let us remember how hard it is, in religion as in
politics, to tell what is going on beneath the surface of
events. Thus, what took place at Runnymede in 1215 was
that King John, much against his royal will, signed Magna
Carta. (This laid it down that no man could be punished
without a fair trial, and no new taxes imposed without the
consent of the people.) When King John signed the
charter, few could have seen what was really going on.
Now, with the benefit of hindsight, we can see that what
was being inaugurated was British parliamentary
democracy as we know it today.

So it was in the first century AD when Jesus came into
Galilee proclaiming, 'The time has come; the kingdom of
God is upon you; repent and believe the gospel' (*Mark*
1:14f, *NEB*). He was announcing that God's great saving
action, so long hoped and prayed for, was now beginning.

Few, if any, could have guessed that one of history's great turning-points had been reached.

So, in two parables, Jesus gave his hearers a hint of what God was really doing.

The reign of God, he said, is like what happens to a housewife when she buries a bit of yeast in 'three measures (i.e. half a hundredweight) of flour' (*NEB*).⁵ If you have ever seen leaven at work, under a microscope, you will know what he meant. What happens is a small explosion, all bubbles and eruptions, which does not stop till the whole batch of flour is leavened (*Matthew* 13:33, Q).

Just so, says Jesus, when God's reign enters history it sets up a dynamic disturbance which no age or society can escape.

Now consider that other parable, the Mustard Seed, in which Jesus hinted to his hearers at what was going on beneath the surface of events (*Mark* 4:30-32; *Matthew* 13:31f, *Luke* 13:18f).

For long, among the Jews, the mustard seed had been proverbial for the smallest thing imaginable. 'Have you ever noticed', asked Jesus, 'that commonplace miracle in nature which can transform a tiny mustard seed into a shrub ten feet tall in which "the birds of the air" (i.e. the wild birds) make their dwellings? This miracle is now beginning to happen in the spiritual world.'

'The birds of the air' was a familiar Jewish nickname for the Gentiles, as in the Old Testament the tree in whose branches the wild birds make their nests symbolised a world-wide empire (*Daniel* 4:12, *Ezekiel* 17:22f).

Even so, said Jesus, the reign of God which may now seem a thing of infinitesimal importance, is destined to span the earth and include in it the Gentiles from afar.

Small beginnings, great endings—this is the point of both parables. What have they to say to us?

Today there is no shortage of human sin and devilry, so that even Christians sometimes fear for the future of God's cause in the world. It is here that Christ's two parables ought to put faith and hope into the faint-hearted. In the mind and purpose of God to whom 'a thousand years are as one day', is nineteen hundred years really a long time?

I once received a letter from the Queen (now the Queen Mother) who had read a book of mine. She began by confessing that she had read its last chapter, which was about the resurrection, first. 'It was dreadful cheating', she went on, 'but it makes a wonderful and hopeful background to the whole book, and I don't regret it.' Then she said, 'What a short time is nineteen hundred years! Perhaps the light of the resurrection will yet flood the world.'

Oh, if only the faint-hearted would read history with the Queen Mother's eyes! Nineteen hundred years have come and gone since the planting of the mustard seed and the putting-in of the leaven, and we are far from seeing the end of it all, or grasping the true Christian situation today.

Here in Britain where Church membership declines in our sick society, we forget what is happening elsewhere:

> For while the tired waves, vainly breaking,
>> Seem here no painful inch to gain,
> Far back, through creeks and inlets making,
>> Comes silent, flooding in, the main.

The spiritual malaise of this island is no true index to the health of the Christian cause in the world today. Even in communist Russia, and spite of all anti-God propaganda, there are fifty million Christians. 'The great new fact of our time' (in William Temple's phrase) is that Christ's Church now has outposts in most corners of the earth, numbers more than a thousand millions, and is gaining thousands of new converts every day.

So, lift up your hearts, all you little-faiths! Only a small part of the scroll of history is yet unrolled. The new dawn which arose in Galilee almost two thousand years ago has yet greater splendours to unfold. 'We are really the early Christians', as Temple put it, and we have God's great future, and hereafter, before us.

IV

Now turn to the parables of the Hidden Treasure and the Precious Pearl (*Matthew* 13:44ff).

But, first, a modern parallel. In the Spring of 1947, when two Arab lads were tending their flocks down near the Dead Sea, one animal went missing. Searching for it, one boy threw a stone into a small cave in the cliff face. When he heard what sounded like breaking crockery, he took sudden fright. Later, the two lads crept into the cave; and there, on its floor, stuffed in long jars, behold roll upon roll of crumbling leather. They had found the famous Dead Sea Scrolls. Nineteen hundred years before, some miles to the north, Jesus, proclaiming the good news of God's dawning kingdom, told a similar story about the chance discovery of a treasure trove. A farmer was ploughing a field when, suddenly, the coulter laid bare a cache of precious coins which, years before, someone had hidden to preserve it from robbers or advancing armies. Making sure no-one had seen him, he shovelled back the earth on the treasure, and hurried home to scrape up every penny to buy that field.

On another occasion, Jesus told a story about a trader whose business was the search for fine pearls. One day he got news of the sort of pearl he had been seeking for years. Without more ado he sold all his assets and purchased that marvellous pearl.

The point of both these parables is the same: 'How

precious is a place in God's kingdom! Is not such blessedness worth any sacrifice?'

Now come down two or three centuries to the early Church, with written gospels before them and scholars busily interpreting the words 'that will never pass away'. To our surprise, we find them identifying the pearl and the treasure not with the kingdom of God but with Christ himself. Yet, come to think of it, they were not wrong. You cannot read the gospels intelligently without perceiving that to follow Christ is to be *in* the kingdom of God, that it is where he is, that in fact he *embodies* it. This is why, after the resurrection, the apostles preached Christ rather than the kingdom. The gospel of the kingdom is Christ in essence; Christ risen from the dead is the gospel of the kingdom come with power. He is the truth of his own greatest gospel. (As Karl Barth put it, 'Jesus Christ spoke of the kingdom of God, and he *was* the kingdom of God.')

Now come down to the twentieth century and ourselves.

The world contains many religions, with doubtless a grain of God's truth in all of them since, in all generations, God has not left men without 'some clue to his nature', as Paul said (*Acts* 14:17). But, when 'the chips are really down'—when it is not an armchair argument or a debating society but the matter of a faith to live by in this dark and sinful world—what else, nay, who else is there but the Christ in whom countless Christians have found God's hidden treasure and precious pearl embodied in a man?

In Christ, Paul told the Colossians, are hid all God's 'treasures of wisdom and knowledge' (*Colossians* 2:3). It is still true. Here in Christ incarnate, crucified, risen, exalted and now, through the Holy Spirit, present with us, is all that the heart of religious man could desire: the assurance through his cross of God's forgiveness for guilty men; the 'living hope' of immortal life through his victory over death; the promise of new beginnings for all who have made shipwreck of their lives; and a kingdom which summons us to service among our fellow-men and which is invincible and everlasting.

Is not this spiritual wealth which demonetises all other currencies? Is not this heavenly treasure which will last on when all earthly treasures disintegrate through inflation or economic slump?

All this, it seems to us, is the spiritual lesson for today of our two tiny parables.

V

Now, finally, let us study what is, by universal consent, the supreme parable. 'The Prodigal Son' we call it, but we shall see that there is good reason for re-naming it (*Luke* 15:11-32).

According to Luke, it began as a verbal riposte, or sword-thrust, in Christ's clash with the Scribes and Pharisees who complained that he was opening the gates of God's kingdom to the outcasts and rejects of society. But how do we interpret it?

The simplest explanation of the story, and the only one which makes sense of it, is that the father represents God, the elder brother the censorious Scribes and Pharisees, and the younger brother the tax-gatherers and sinners whom Jesus befriended. Therefore in the parable God, by the lips of Jesus, declares his free forgiveness for penitent sinners while at the same time gently rebuking the self-righteous Pharisees.

If so, our traditional name for the parable is a

misnomer, for the chief character in the story is neither of the two sons. It is the father. Right up to the very last scene, his meeting with the disgruntled elder brother, he broods over the whole story. Call it then 'the parable of the father's love' or 'the waiting father'. It does not matter, for the father waits because he loves and the father represents God.

We saw earlier that Jesus' parables are generally stories from real life. To this rule our parable seems no exception. They had prodigal sons in Jesus' day. We still have them today. In the same way, every generation has its 'far country', and one of its names today is 'Hippie Land'.

But if this is a story from real life, it is also far more. Some have taken Jesus to be saying in the parable, 'This is how an earthly father would treat his returning prodigal. And will not the good Father above?' But is this, in fact, how ordinary human fathers generally welcome home their returning prodigals? Do they really run to meet them, embrace and kiss them, load them with expensive presents and new clothes, and reward them with a barbecue and a ball?

You may have heard of the modern prodigal who, on turning up in the 'far country' of a neighbouring parish was advised by the local minister to go back home, and his father would kill the fatted calf for him. The prodigal did so. Later, meeting the minister again, he was asked hopefully, 'Well, and did he kill the fatted calf for you?' 'No', came the rueful reply, 'but he nearly killed the prodigal son.'

Who will deny that it often happens thus in real life, even in this 'permissive age'?

The point is that Jesus' story is *larger than life*. The father of the prodigal is not an ordinary father, but a quite extraordinary one. What Jesus is here depicting is the great grace of God—his goodness going beyond all justice—to undeserving men.

VI

How are we to put across the truth of this parable to men today?[6]

Let the younger son stand for all those today who, 'fed up' with the establishment and impatient of 'law and order', rebel against them and resolve to have their fling.

Likewise, let the elder son stand for all the unadventurous, conventional Christians, who turn a cold disliking eye on all their rebellious contemporaries.

To those stay-at-home Christians who complain that they have always done what they should but have never had any 'bright lights' in their lives, the father of the parable (who is God) is saying, 'Son, you are always with me, and all that is mine is yours.' In other words, if you happen to be in the elder brother's shoes, give God thanks for the blessings which you so lightly take for granted and be grateful that you have escaped all the heartache and hopelessness of your prodigal contemporaries.

And to our modern prodigals the father is saying, 'You chose freedom, and I didn't stop you. All the time you have been in the far country I have been worrying about you. And here I am, still waiting to welcome you home.'

For the perennial truth of this parable is that behind the drift and destiny of human affairs, and brooding over them in infinite compassion is a holy, heavenly Father. And, as Augustine, the greatest returned prodigal of all, declared, 'Thou hast made us for thyself and our heart is restless, until it finds its rest in thee.'

Thus, the last secret of the parable is this: there may be a home-coming for us all, because there is a home. The door of the kingdom which leads to our Father's house with its many rooms (*John* 14:2) still stands wide open, as there is One who has died to open it to sinners, and who still says 'I am the true and living way to the Father' (*John* 14:6).

The decisive, existential question for us is, 'Do we want to come home?' For, as P T Forsyth put it, summing up all the long debate about predestination and free will, 'We are all predestined, in love, to life, sooner or later—if we will.'[7]

NOTES

1. For example, in the parable of the Sower, sowing precedes ploughing, the precise opposite of our practice in the West.

2. Great speakers and teachers have rightly used hyperbole in order to stab us lesser men wide awake to matters of great moment. Arthur Balfour, the British statesman, once said to Winston Churchill: 'I admire the exaggerated way in which you tell the truth.'

3. Charles W. F. Smith, *The Jesus of the Parables*, p 16.

4. 'Perfection beyond compare' Lord Tennyson called them.

5. The parable implies a baking big enough to feed a hundred and fifty hungry mouths. No ordinary housewife, in her senses, would bake such an enormous quantity. In other words, we are dealing here with no ordinary human situation but with an extraordinary divine reality; with what the sovereign power of God can really do.

6. See H. Thielicke's *The Waiting Father*, pp 17ff.

7. P. T. Forsyth, *This Life and the Next*, p 16.

Chapter 4

The Kingdom and the Cross

Calvary, not Bethlehem, is the chief place of divine revelation in the New Testament. The cross which ended his earthly life, rather than the cradle where it began, holds the secret of the Lord. It was the cross which crowned his earthly mission, and of which he cried triumphantly before he died, 'The work is done!' (*tetelestai*, *John* 19:30).

I

What 'work' was this? Consider first three titles which contain the key to what he was and did: Son of God, Son of man, and Servant of the Lord.

As we have seen, the deepest secret of his life was his awareness of being God's only Son. Going back apparently to his boyhood (*Luke* 2:49), it is heard in his address to God as 'Father' (*Abba*), or 'my Father', and finds supreme expression in his great thanksgiving (*Matthew* 11:25f, Q).

Only to his disciples, however, did Jesus disclose this secret. In public, he chose to be known as 'the Son of man'. This cryptic title, derived from the famous vision in *Daniel* 7, Jesus applied to himself as the head of the new people of God, now on earth humiliated but destined to be exalted into the presence of God (*Mark* 14:62).

It was another Old Testament figure, Isaiah's Servant of the Lord (see especially *Isaiah* 42:1-9 and 53), which showed Jesus the way he must travel if God's work were to be done.

41

This work—his 'ministry' we call it—had its prelude when, identifying himself with sinners, he went down from Nazareth and submitted to John's baptism in Jordan (*Mark* 1:9-13). Observe how in Mark's account Jewish images are used to express heavenly realities imperceptible to outward eye and ear. It is idle to ask what actually happened if by this you mean, could it have been photographed or recorded on tape. Yet it was, as we say, 'an historic occasion', a crucial moment in that traffic between two worlds which holds the key to his whole spiritual life.

The descent of the Spirit on Jesus means that he knows himself to be equipped with divine power for his work (cf *Isaiah* 42:1, 'I have put my Spirit upon him'). The voice sounding in his soul, 'Thou art my only Son', authenticates his divine sonship. 'On thee my favour rests', echoes Isaiah's Servant of the Lord: 'My chosen, in whom I delight' (*Isaiah* 42:1). Thus, the Son of man is marked out at his baptism as the Servant-Son of God.

When news came that Herod Antipas had imprisoned his fore-runner, John the Baptist, Jesus knew that his time had come.

Into Galilee he came announcing that the decisive hour of history had struck, God's rule had begun, and men must 'turn back' to God and make his good news their own. With authority he began to teach in their synagogues (e.g. at Nazareth, *Luke* 4:16ff): in the towns he wrought miracles of healing, so that his fame ran through all Galilee and beyond.

But his consorting with notorious sinners and outcasts, his claim to forgive sins, i.e. to be the divine pardon incarnate, and his 'cavalier' attitude to the sacred Sabbath so shocked the Jewish churchmen that, in order to continue his work, he had to quit the synagogues for the lakeside. Thus Jesus spearheaded his great campaign, the kingdom of God against the powers of evil, as by parables he challenged his hearers with the claims of the kingdom and by miracles of mercy manifested its presence.

Twelve men whom he had trained to be the nucleus of the new Israel he now dispatched to proclaim God's dawning rule by word and deed. So high did the popular excitement run after their return from this mission, that thousands thronged after Jesus to the north end of the Lake. There, in a desert place, he fed them with the bread of the kingdom. It was the Galilean Lord's Supper. He had come not to invite the righteous but sinners to the banquet of God's kingdom (*Mark* 2:17); and there he was now doing it, acting out his own parable of the Great Supper (*Luke* 14:16-24), hopeful that, by their response, the Galileans would align themselves with God's great purpose incarnate in himself.

Alas, by their reactions, the five thousand men betrayed how earth-bound were their notions of God's Kingdom and Messiah. What they were dreaming of was 'a revolt in the desert' against hated Rome, with Jesus as its leader (*John* 6:15).

Long before, in the wilderness (*Matthew* 4:8-10, Q), Jesus had rejected this sort of Messiahship as a very temptation of the devil. So now, briefly, he escaped from the dangerous enthusiasm of his followers, outside of Galilee (*Mark* 7:24), that in quiet communion with his Father he might learn the divine will for himself. By the time he and the Twelve had reached Caesarea Philippi, he knew.

Messiah he was, as Peter now confessed him to be, but a Messiah who *must*, as the Lord's Servant, go to his throne by way of a gibbet (*Mark* 8:31). 'Your Messiah', he told the protesting Peter, 'is a conqueror. God's Messiah is a Servant.' If God's rule were to be effectuated

'in power' (*Mark* 9:1), a *via dolorosa* (way of the cross)
stretched out before him and his.

Six days later, there occurred on 'a high mountain'
(probably Hermon) the Transfiguration (*Mark* 9:2-13;
Luke 9:28-36). As Jesus prayed, the rapture of his communion with his Father apparently irradiated his whole
person and, in a state midway between sleep and waking,
Peter, James and John had a vision in which Jesus talked
with Moses and Elijah.

Was this vision the counterpart in the disciples'
experience of their Master's at his baptism, and meant to
confirm to them the truth disclosed to them at Caesarea
Philippi? Or, if we ask what happened to Jesus on the
mountain top, may we say that his true spiritual nature
broke through the limitations of his humanity and was
revealed by God in vision to his three disciples?

At any rate, Jesus now set his face towards Jerusalem
for an 'exodus' (*Luke* 9:30) which would deliver men from
a greater bondage than that of Egypt.

There followed a ministry of some three months in
Jerusalem[1] (*John* 7:10-10:40), in which Jesus challenged
Israel's rulers with the divine crisis now overhanging
God's ancient people and summoning them to repent
before it was too late. (This is the background of many of
his parables of crisis, e.g. the Barren Fig Tree, On the
Way to Court, the Traveller at Sunset, the Shut Door,
the Wicked Tenants etc[2]). As opposition to him mounted,
Jesus met it as he had met an earlier crisis in Galilee, by
withdrawing, this time across the Jordan (*John* 10:40).
There, in Transjordan, his purpose crystallised in the
decision to return to Jerusalem at the approaching
Passover. (This is the 'life-setting' of the 'Q' saying,
Luke 13:35. Probably uttered as he withdrew, it is an
announcement that he will return at Passover.)

Then ensued all the events we associate with Holy Week: the entry into Jerusalem, the cleansing of the Temple, the priests' plot and the betrayal, the arrest and the trial, the crucifixion and the burial. For a moment in Gethsemane he seemed to hesitate and there was an hour of agony. But on he went to the end of the road marked out for the Servant of God and, by and by, on an April Sunday morning (in AD 30), came back in glory to his disciples and commissioned them for their future work.

II

Of Jesus' passion it has been said that he was a traveller by faith rather than one who clearly sees the end from the beginning. Nonetheless, on the road which took him from Galilee to Golgotha, he gave his disciples hint after pregnant hint of the purpose of his mission and the blessings it would bring.

Here are four metaphors which he employed: (1) 'I have a baptism to undergo' (*Luke* 12:50; *Mark* 10:38). His passion was a baptism in blood which would cleanse men from their sins (cf. *I John* 1:7). (2) It was a 'cup' of suffering which his Father had given him to drink, so that there might be established a 'new covenant' between God and sinful men (*Mark* 10:38, 14:23f; *I Corinthians* 11:25). (3) Once, Jesus likened his passion to a road to be travelled: 'The Son of man', he said, 'is going the way appointed for him in the scriptures' (*Mark* 14:21 *NEB*; the reference must be to *Isaiah* 53). (4) Not far from the end he told his followers, 'The Son of man came not to be served but to serve and to give his life as a ransom for many' (*Mark* 10:45, where 'many' is idiomatic Hebrew for 'all', and again *Isaiah* 53 is in the background). His death was the price that had to be paid if they were to be delivered from the doom which overhung them.

So, by one vivid figure after another, Jesus signalled at the meaning and purpose of his 'work' before he finished it on the cross.

In the literal sense of the word, the cross was not a sacrifice but a miscarriage of justice brought about by Jew and Roman acting in their own self-interest. But, as John Ruskin finely said, 'the great mystery of the idea of sacrifice itself is that you cannot save men from death but by facing it for them, nor from sin but by resisting it for them.'[3] In this sense, Jesus' death *was* a sacrifice. It was his readiness to accept what others forced on him and to see it as a sacrifice he could offer to God which transformed an act of human sin into an act of divine redemption. In the cross we find the supreme instance of Joseph's words to his brothers: 'As for you, you meant evil against me; but God meant it for good, to bring it about that many people should be kept alive' (*Genesis* 50:20 *RSV*).

So we may see how 'man proposes but God disposes', how things willed by sinful men are yet used by God and, by a stroke of divine irony, man's greatest crime turns into God's greatest blessing.

It is worth remembering that, if the disciples' last sight of their Master had been of him hanging on a cross, these passion sayings we have been quoting would never have been remembered, nor possibly Jesus himself. It was the resurrection and the coming of the Holy Spirit which taught his followers to see the cross not as stark tragedy brought about by men who 'knew not that they did', but as the divine way of making sinners 'one with the goodness of God himself' (*2 Corinthians* 5:21, *NEB*).

III

To the Jews a 'stumbling-block' and to the Greeks 'folly', so Paul describes their reactions to the cross (*I*

Corinthians 1:23); yet in the same letter he also records how, within half a dozen years, Christ's apostles had reached a common finding about the meaning of the cross: 'Christ died for our sins according to the scriptures' (*I Corinthians* 15:3ff). Chief among those 'scriptures' must have been *Isaiah* 53 which tells of God's suffering Servant who 'bore the sin of many'.

Yet each of the apostolic writers saw the cross from his own particular angle.

When in *Acts* 3 and 4 and in his first letter (*I Peter* 2: 21-25) we find Peter identifying his living Lord with 'God's Servant', we perceive that he has now grasped the truth from which at Caesarea Philippi he had once recoiled in horror (*Mark* 8:32f).

Among the apostles, however, it was not Peter the rough fisherman but Paul the trained theological thinker who penetrated most deeply into the mystery of the cross. Once, in *Romans* 3:25, he says that Christ crucified has become for all men what the 'mercy seat' (see *Exodus* 25:16-22) symbolised for old Israel, the place where God draws near and shows his mercy to sinners. Yet perhaps Paul's profoundest word about the cross comes in *2 Corinthians* 5:21 where, explaining how God 'made Christ sin' for our sakes, he depicts the cross as an act wherein, by God's appointing, our condemnation came upon the sinless Christ that for us there might be 'condemnation no more'.

For John, Christ is 'the Lamb of God who takes away the world's sin' (*John* 1:29). He 'dies to make men holy' (*John* 17:19). He acts—'I now sanctify myself'; men are acted on—'that they too may be sanctified', i.e. that by his blood they may be cleansed from sin (*I John* 1:7).

In *Hebrews*, Christ is portrayed as our great and merciful High Priest who, by the offering of his own sinless life in obedience to God's will, has opened up for us 'a new and living way' into the holy of holies, which is heaven (*Hebrews* 10:1-22).

Finally, John, the seer of Patmos, speaks for all early Christians in his doxology to Christ: 'Now to him who loves us and has loosed us from our sins by his own blood' (*Revelation* 1:5).

So, through the apostolic writings runs one mighty thought: Christ died for our sins, bore what we should have borne, did for us what was God's good pleasure, did for us what we could never have done for ourselves. Bunyan's Pilgrim summed it up: 'He hath given me rest by his sorrow and life by his death.'

IV

Theology is simply 'faith thinking', faith giving a reasoned account of itself. Down nineteen centuries the best minds of the Church have sought to interpret the cross to their contemporaries in ways they could understand. To what conclusions have they come?

All have agreed that *the cross reveals the love of God* (*John* 3:16, *I John* 4:10, *Romans* 5:8). No Christian would deny this. It finds expression in what Matthew Arnold called the greatest hymn in the English language, Isaac Watts's 'When I survey the wondrous Cross'. Yet, if we take this to be the whole truth, we come short of 'the mind of Christ' who knew himself called not simply to *reveal* God's love but to *do* something for men which they could never have done for themselves.

So, second, most Christian thinkers have agreed with the apostles that *Christ bore our sins*. But how? By so identifying himself with the race he came to save that he entered with us, and for us, into the divine judgment that must ever rest upon the sin of man. The 'cup' Christ had

to drink was 'the cup our sins had mingled', and in the
agony of Gethsemane and the dereliction of the cross he is
to be seen drinking it to the bitter dregs.

Some have said that in all this God was 'punishing'
Jesus in our stead. Put thus, it is a revolting idea. Were a
human judge so to allow an innocent man to be punished
for another's crime, we should unhesitatingly call him
'unjust'. No more should we so describe God's treatment
of a Son who was ever well-pleasing to him.

'Penal' Christ's sufferings were, but only in the sense
that in his passion he had to endure on men's behalf the
divine reaction against the sin of the race to whom he had
betrothed himself for better, for worse. If we think of the
suffering which good men often endure when they deeply
love wrongdoers, we may surmise how Jesus felt as he
went to the cross. We may also perceive that, in so
identifying himself with sinners, he was honouring the
holiness of God who, just because of his love for them,
cannot condone sin but must deal with it, if they are to be
forgiven.

Even so, we have not yet mentioned what is perhaps the
highest thing ever said about the cross. Since, for
Christians, 'the Judge of all the earth' is a heavenly Father
who wills that his wayward children should return to their
Father's house, no mere law-court language can take us to
the full truth. Legal categories must make way for
personal and moral ones.

Adopting them, we may see Christ in his work as *the
great confessor of our sins before his Father*. Thus John
McLeod Campbell saw the cross in his classic book *The
Nature of the Atonement* (1856). Christ, he said, offered,
as our representative on the cross, a perfect confession of
our sins, a confession which could be described as 'a
perfect Amen in humanity to the judgment of God on the

sin of man'. To the divine wrath against sin Christ responded, on man's behalf, 'Righteous art Thou, O Lord, who judgest so.' And by that perfect response he absorbed it, so making possible our forgiveness by holy God.

If somebody should object to this doctrine, 'Nobody can confess sin but the sinner himself—how then could the sinless Christ confess our sins?', we may reply: 'A human mother can make her own the sin of her child, and could not Christ have done this for the race he came to save?' If the sin of other people can be so felt, it can also be confessed, not indeed as our own, but as that of those whom we love. And had not our Lord so betrothed himself to the human race for better, for worse?

'No man is an island', said John Donne. Human beings are not separate entities, like pebbles on a beach. We are all bound up together in the bundle of life. Nowadays we are realising afresh what Paul realised long ago, namely, the truly *corporate* nature of sin. As Reinhold Niebuhr said, moral man finds himself entangled in an immoral society. Willy nilly, we are all caught up in the mesh of the world's wickedness.

So we may understand how Christ, though himself sinless, had, in becoming man, so deeply involved himself in our sin that from the inside (as it were) he could perfectly confess our sins to his Father.

We do well then to see the cross as a revelation of God's love. We do better to think of the atonement as an act in which Christ entered with us, and for us, into God's judgment on sin, so removing the barrier which separated us from him. We do best of all to think of Christ as representing us before his Father and making, as only he could make, a perfect confession of our sins, thus enabling us, in Paul's phrase, to be 'accepted in the Beloved' (*Ephesians* 1:6).

After all this 'theologising' let us sum up in a homely parable: You and I are like the boy who has misbehaved and been sent to his room in disgrace. There he sits, sullen and resentful. Suddenly he becomes aware of his elder brother in the room, apparently sharing his disgrace. 'Surely', he muses, 'he hasn't done wrong also?' Then on his elder brother's face he sees a look which he cannot quite fathom. It almost looks as if his elder brother were really glad to be there. Then the elder brother invites him to go back to their father. The boy refuses. Thereupon the elder brother says, 'All is forgiven. Father will take you back, for my sake.' So, shamefacedly, the boy goes. But when he comes into his father's presence, he catches the same look on his father's face as he had seen on his elder brother's. And the father takes the errant boy into his arms and forgives him.

Such is Christ's work *for* us. Yet, to be effective, it must also become Christ's work *in* us. And this it becomes when we respond to it in humble faith, when round the holy table we partake of 'Christ's love-tokens to his Body the Church' (P. T. Forsyth), and when, in our day-by-day living, we try to serve our fellow men in sacrificial acts of kindness and of love, for his dear sake.

Our forefathers liked to speak of 'the finished work of Christ', and rightly. In principle, this sinful world has been redeemed: the thing is done, it is not to do. In a true sense, the cross was the last judgment, as John represents Christ as saying (*John* 12:31). Yet no doctrine of the atonement is complete which has not a 'forward look'. The redemption once for all wrought on the cross remains to be worked out until, as the early Christians sang, 'At the name of Jesus every knee shall bow, to God the Father's praise' (*Philippians* 2:10).

We have been summarising Christian thinking about

Christ's work. No doctrine of the atonement can express the whole truth of that act wherein God in Christ took the responsibility of evil upon himself and somehow subsumed it under good. Wisely, the Church universal has never required subscription to any particular theory of it as necessary for saving faith.

Yet this does not mean that we should be content to regard the cross as 'a fact without a meaning'. Is there, then, no simple statement about the cross to which most Christians could say 'Amen'? We believe such a statement may be found in three verses of a hymn which an Irish poetess, Cecil Frances Alexander, wrote for children:

> He died that we might be forgiven,
>   He died to make us good,
> That we might go at last to heaven
>   Saved by his precious blood.
>
> There was no other good enough
>   To pay the price of sin,
> He only could unlock the gate
>   Of heaven, and let us in.
>
> O dearly, dearly has he loved,
>   And we must love him too,
> And trust in his redeeming love
>   And try his works to do.

On the redemption, won for us on the cross, God set his seal by raising his Son from the dead. The resurrection is the guarantee of the atonement. It is God's answer to the cry of dereliction. It is the divine 'Yes' to the finished work of Christ. But this is to anticipate the theme of our next chapter.

NOTES

1. On this Jerusalem ministry (telescoped in *Mark*, though implied in *Mark* 14:49) see M. Goguel, *The Life of Jesus*, pp 238-250; C. H. Dodd, *A Companion to the Bible* (Ed T. W. Manson) pp 371f, and V. Taylor, *The Life and Ministry of Jesus*, pp 164ff.

2. See the author's *Interpreting the Parables*, chapter 6.

3. The root idea of sacrifice in the Bible is of an offering with which the worshipper can identify himself in his approach to holy God.

C

Chapter 5

The Resurrection

If the cross was crucial, the resurrection is quite central, as our theologians of hope (Moltmann, Pannenberg etc) have recently insisted. Too long in the west the resurrection has been treated as an appendix to the cross whereas it is in fact its key. Better justice is done it in the liturgies of eastern Christendom, as those people know who have witnessed the pre-Easter ritual of the Orthodox Church which culminates in the tremendous midnight cry, '*Christos anesté!*—Christ is risen!'

The resurrection is in fact the diamond pivot on which the whole truth or falsity of Christianity turns. Long ago Paul told the Corinthians, 'If Christ has not been raised, your faith is futile, and you are still in your sins.' (*I Corinthians* 15:17). No dead Christ can save us. Only a risen and reigning Christ can.

For consider: If the story of Jesus ends at Calvary, it is unmitigated tragedy and the supreme proof of the irrationality of the universe. Let it once be established that that perfect life went out in utter darkness, and we might as well conclude that there is no good and wise heavenly Father but only, in Thomas Hardy's grim phrase, 'a vast Imbecility'. But if the resurrection is true, if God by raising Christ from the dead set his seal upon the work of the cross, why then he is shown to be not only merciful but, as Paul saw and said, invincible (*Romans* 8:31-39).

54

So let us study the resurrection first as historical fact. then as spiritual experience, and finally as immortal hope.

I

First, as historical fact. In an enquiry of this kind it is always a wise rule to discover what, by the judgment of the experts, is the earliest and most reliable evidence.[1] Accordingly, we shall here concentrate on what modern scholars, after critical study, have judged quite clearly to be the oldest and best pieces of evidence for the resurrection, namely, eight verses from a letter of the earliest New Testament writer, Paul, and eight verses from our earliest evangelist, Mark.

The New Testament, we may observe, contains two distinct strands of evidence for the reality of the resurrection. First, we have testimony to various appearances of the risen Lord to his disciples. Second, we have testimony to the fact that on the first Easter Day three women found Joseph of Arimathea's rock-tomb empty. The earliest account of Christ's appearances is, as we shall show, that in *I Corinthians* 15:1-8. The earliest account of the finding of the empty tomb is that in *Mark* 16:1-8. Let us take them in turn.

(1) *I Corinthians* 15:1-8 (*RSV*):

> Now I would remind you, brethren, in what terms I preached to you the gospel . . . ³For I delivered to you as of first importance what I also received, that Christ died for our sins in accordance with the scriptures, ⁴that he was buried, that he was raised on the third day in accordance with the scriptures, ⁵and that he appeared to Cephas, then to the twelve. ⁶Then he appeared to more than five hundred brethren at one time, most of whom are still alive, though some have fallen asleep. ⁷Then he appeared to James, then to all the apostles. ⁸Last of all, as to one untimely born, he appeared also to me.

These are among the most important verses in the New Testament. Observe, first, that most of this passage is something which Paul himself 'received' from those who were Christians before him. Its style proclaims it a very early summary of 'things most surely believed' and that by all the apostles (*I Corinthians* 15:11). Six appearances of the risen Christ are listed: three to individuals, three to groups of people. The words 'most of whom are still alive, though some have fallen asleep' are Paul's added comment, as 'Last of all . . . he appeared also to me' refers to the Damascus Road experience.

Where and when did Paul get this precious 'tradition'? The probable answer is: during his first visit to Jerusalem after his conversion when, as he puts it in *Galatians* 1:18f, he went up 'to get to know Cephas' (i.e. Peter) and stayed a fortnight, in the year AD 35. And this for two good reasons. First, the passage contains un-Pauline phrases and 'Semitisms', i.e. Jewish idioms glimmering through the Greek, and pointing to Jerusalem as a place of origin.[2] Second, the two apostles named in the 'tradition' are precisely the two whom Paul says he met during his fortnight's visit, Peter and James the Lord's brother.

Here is testimony to the fact of the resurrection taking us back to within six years of the event. Remarkable evidence indeed! Rightly has our passage been pronounced 'the earliest document of the Christian Church we possess.'

Moreover, and no less important, it is tradition whose truth was *open to testing*. For when Paul was writing *First Corinthians* about twenty years later, i.e. in AD 55, most of 'the five hundred brethren' still survived and were available for questioning. Altogether, then, *I Corinthians* 15:1-8 preserves uniquely early and verifiable testimony. It meets every demand of historical reliability. Doubt it (somebody has said), and you might as well doubt everything else in the New Testament.

(2) Alongside this tradition we have now to set the separate testimony to the empty tomb, found in its earliest form in *Mark* 16:1-8 (*RSV*):

> When the sabbath was past, Mary Magdalene, Mary the mother of James, and Salome bought spices, so that they might go and anoint him. ²And very early on the first day of the week they went to the tomb when the sun had risen. ³And they were saying to one another, 'Who will roll away the stone for us from the door of the tomb?' ⁴And, looking up, they saw that the stone was rolled back; for it was very large. ⁵And entering the tomb, they saw a young man sitting on the right side, dressed in a white robe; and they were amazed. ⁶And he said to them, "Do not be amazed; you seek Jesus of Nazareth, who was crucified. He has risen; he is not here; see the place where they laid him. ⁷But go, tell his disciples and Peter that he is going before you to Galilee; there you will see him, as he told you.' ⁸And they went out and fled from the tomb; for trembling and astonishment had come upon them; and they said nothing to anyone, for they were afraid . . .

The first part of the story of Jesus to be written down was not (as might be supposed) that of his birth but that of his cross and resurrection.[3] Our passage, *Mark* 16:1-8, is the climax of just such an account, most probably based on Peter's testimony and very early indeed.

A study of its contents confirms this. The narrative has a convincing sobriety and matter-of-factness. Next, if it had not in fact been true, no Jew would have made three *women*, not disciples, the first recipients of the news that the tomb was empty. Women's witness in those days was poorly regarded.[4] Verse 3 ('They were wondering among themselves who would roll away the stone', *NEB*) suggests their vividly remembered perplexity. The words in verse 7, 'Go and tell the disciples *and Peter*', have the ring of authenticity. After Peter's denial of Jesus, he needed just such an assurance that he was not cast off. Finally, the statement in verse 8 that the women fled from the tomb in what we would call 'numinous terror' was surely never fabricated. It suggests the awesomeness and mystery of the sight which met their gaze. Thus, 'if we test what is here capable of being tested, we cannot shake Mark's story of the empty tomb.'[5]

We have, then, two strong strands of historical evidence for the resurrection. Both go back almost to the beginnings of Christianity. But the important thing to note is that *they originated independently*. The story of the empty tomb in *Mark* 16 does not record an appearance of the risen Christ, and concerns not disciples but three women. On the other hand, the record of his appearances had originally no connection with the locality of the grave. Granted to disciples, they were in the nature of calls to apostolic mission. Thus, our two independent strands *complement and confirm each other*, and show that belief in Christ's resurrection is rooted not in fantasy but in historical fact.

But this evidence does not stand alone. To its truth there are four great witnesses:

First, the change in the life of the disciples. Before the resurrection, like frightened sheep, 'they all forsook him and fled' (*Mark* 14:50). After the resurrection they were as bold as lions.

Second, the Church. Had the crucifixion ended the disciples' fellowship with Jesus, it is hard to see how the Church could ever have come into existence, and harder still to explain how it has lasted two thousand years.

Third, the New Testament itself. Who would have troubled to write these twenty-seven books if Jesus' career had ended on the cross? Every written record about him was made by men who believed in a risen Lord.

Fourth, the Lord's Day. No Christian Jew would have changed the sacred day from Sabbath (Saturday) to 'the first day of the week' (*Acts* 20:7; *I Corinthians* 16:2;

Revelation 1:10) except for the reason that on this day Jesus was known to have triumphed over death.

II

We have now to consider the *nature* of Christ's resurrection. In *I Corinthians* 15 Paul declares that a change from a 'natural' to a 'spiritual' (or 'heavenly') body is the destiny of the Christian believer and, since he calls Christ 'the *first-fruits* of those who have fallen asleep', he plainly believed the same wonderful change to have come over Christ's body at the resurrection: his 'lowly' body had become 'the body of glory' (*Philippians* 3:21).

Next, because, in *I Corinthians* 15:1-8, Paul ranks his sight of the risen Lord with that of Peter, James and the others, we naturally and rightly infer that *they held the same view*. For them, Christ was already in the unseen world of God, from which, in his glorified body, he had manifested himself to them. The appearances recorded in *I Corinthians* 15 are therefore 'disclosures from heaven' of the already exalted Christ. For the earliest Christians resurrection and ascension were not two events but one. (Only in *Acts* 1:1-11 do we have the suggestion that they were separate events.).

From the earliest evidence we therefore conclude that Christ must have left the grave 'incorruptibly', his earthly body having been transmuted into a heavenly one. Consistent with this would be the closely detailed description of the grave-clothes, suggesting the testimony of an eye-witness, in *John* 20:6f. The wording suggests that Jesus' physical body had passed out of its wrappings into what Paul called a 'spiritual' and glorified body, without deranging the grave-clothes which had lapsed back into their original places.[6]

What, finally, did the fact of the resurrection mean for

the first Christians? On the day of Pentecost Peter said, 'Let all Israel accept as certain that God made this Jesus, whom you crucified, both Lord and Messiah' (*Acts* 2:36 *NEB*). When Jesus hazarded all upon his faith in God, nature had echoed and rung to his venture; God had said 'Yes' to the work ended on the cross. The ministry was not finished; it was going on, but now with a Christ let loose in the earth where neither Caiaphas nor Pilate could stop his truth. Not chance but divine love was on the throne of the universe.

Yet for Jews, for such the first Christians were, it meant even more. For them (compare Martha's words in *John* 11:24) 'the resurrection of the dead' was the great hope of the End-time when God would wind up the scroll of history and there would follow the last judgment. But, if Jesus had been raised from the dead, then in one Man—and the cause which he embodied—that end had been marvellously anticipated. Small wonder then that the first Christians felt themselves to be living in a new age, as that 'one vacant tomb in the wide graveyard of the world' was for them the first and glorious instalment of God's future for his people![7]

III

The fact of the resurrection does not however stand alone. We must, secondly, reckon with the *experience*; men's spiritual experience of the risen Christ down the centuries.

If, as we have seen, Christ did not return to his former life, he had not forsaken his followers. James Denney once said, paradoxically, that 'no apostle ever remembered Christ'. The paradox is true. The apostles had no need to. On the contrary, through the coming of the Holy Spirit, Jesus' *alter ego*, he was still with them, as the *Book of Acts* shows. The presence of the Holy Spirit, and he is the chief actor in this our earliest church history-book, is in fact Jesus' own presence in spirit, through whom Christians believe themselves to be sharing in his risen life.

Today there exists at Mirfield in Yorkshire an Anglican brotherhood called 'the Community of the Resurrection'. But nineteen centuries earlier Paul was describing his churches as 'communities of the resurrection'. 'If then you have been raised with Christ', he writes to the Christians in Colossae, 'seek the things that are above where Christ is, seated at the right hand of God' (*Colossians* 3:1).[8] Or, he tells the Ephesians, 'God, rich in mercy, brought us to life with Christ, even when we were dead in our sins, and in union with Christ Jesus raised us up and enthroned us with him in the heavenly realms.' (*Ephesians* 2:4ff, *NEB*). Somehow it is a matter of heaven on earth, here and now:

> The men of grace have found
> Glory begun below.

(When John writes about 'life' or 'eternal life'—and they mean the same thing—he is referring to a like experience. 'God gave us eternal life', he says, 'and this life is in his Son. He who has the Son has life.' (*I John* 5:11f).

Moreover, all down the Christian centuries this experience has been repeated. From Polycarp of Smyrna to David Livingstone in 'darkest Africa', from Dr Dale of Birmingham to Sir William Grenfell of Labrador (and how many more might be named!) the testimony has been the same: 'Christ is alive! He has had dealings with us, and we with him.'

Nor has the experience been confined to individual great Christians or to professedly Christian countries.

Thus, to take a modern example, in his book *A Faith for this one world* Lesslie Newbigin tells how in the

nineteen-twenties the atheistical Communist Bukharin
went from Moscow to Kiev to address an anti-God rally.
Bukharin proceeded to ridicule the Christian faith till there
seemed no stone left in its edifice. Then questions were
invited. Whereupon a priest of the Orthodox Church
asked leave to speak. Standing beside the Communist, he
faced the people, and across the great hall shouted the
age-old and familiar Easter greeting, 'Christ is risen!' At
once, says Newbigin, 'the whole vast assembly rose to its
feet, and the reply came back like the crash of breakers
against the cliff: "He is risen indeed!" There was no more
reply. There could not be.'

Just so countless Christians in many lands today 'know
that their Redeemer lives' and that they 'are risen with
him' into 'newness of life' (*Romans* 6:4).

IV

Thirdly, the resurrection is a *hope*—our hope founded on
the living Christ. Because he lives, we hope to live also
(*John* 14:19).

Consider what the apostles teach. Whether it is Paul,
Peter, John, the author of *Hebrews* or the seer of Patmos,
all centre their hope of everlasting life in the Christ who
died for them and is now alive for evermore. And what
they believe in is not the immortality of the soul but the
resurrection of the body.

The doctrine of the immortality of the soul is really a
refined form of primitive man's 'animism', that is, his
belief that certain material objects like trees and stones are
possessed by spirits.[9] The Christian doctrine of the
resurrection of the body is founded four-square on
Christ's resurrection and the hope of life hereafter as
God's gift in his risen Son.

For too long many of us Christians have conceived the

future life in Greek, and not biblical, thought-forms. We have thought of man, as Plato did, as an immortal soul encased in a corruptible body.[10] But, as psychologists and doctors nowadays alike hold man's body and mind to be a unity (a psychosomatic whole), so the New Testament, refusing to split man in two, affirms that the life beyond involves the whole person.

Moreover, as recent theologians have pointed out, though the word 'resurrection' comes from the strange world of Jewish apocalyptic, it is simply a metaphor from the familiar experience of re-awakening to the life of a new day and, for the Hebrews, this was a parable of the destiny appointed for God's people at the End-time (Cf *Isaiah* 26:19; *Daniel* 12:2, and *John* 11:24).

But there is a third point to be underlined. Many of our Christian forefathers, dear Isaac Walton of *Compleat Angler* fame among them, in spite of *I Corinthians* 15:50 ('Flesh and blood cannot inherit the kingdom of God'), believed in 'a resurrection of relics'.[11] In actual fact, what the New Testament teaches is a resurrection not of matter but of form. (The 'body' (*sōma*) is the principle of individuation which persists through all changes of substance, so that 'the spiritual body' in the life to come will be one in which the fulness of personality will be preserved.)

'In Adam all die.' We have no biblical warrant for believing that man was created immortal. It is our Christian faith that, when we have 'shuffled off this mortal coil', God will give us new and 'glorious' bodies like that which he gave his Son at the first Easter Day. The Christian hope is that those who are now 'in Christ', grafted by faith into him as the branch is grafted into the living tree, will one day be 'with Christ' (*I Thessalonians* 4:14; *Romans* 8:11). As on the first Easter Day God awakened his Son from the sleep of death, so he will rouse from their last sleep those who are Christ's, and they will rise to make their abode with him in his Father's house (*John* 14:2).

Lastly, the Christian's destiny is nothing less than Christ-likeness. 'We are to be shaped to the likeness of God's Son', says Paul (*Romans* 8:29, *NEB*). Says John, 'We are God's children now, and it does not yet appear what we shall be; but we know that when he appears we shall be like him, for we shall see him as he is.' (*I John* 3:2). Men have painted many and diverse pictures of the after-life, some crude, some carnal, some sentimental. The apostles hold fast what is characteristically Christian: salvation full and final means sharing the likeness of our Lord.

Note on the Ascension (Acts 1:1-11)

For the early Christians, as we have seen, the risen Christ was with God in heaven; and whenever he appears, he comes from heaven and returns there. Only Luke treats the ascension as a separate event. Yet his real concern is not with 'a journey through the skies to a local heaven'. (It is our naiveté, not Luke's, which makes us take literally the 'cloud' of *Acts* 1:9. The cloud is the *shekinah*, the cloud of glory, signifying God's presence.) For Luke, the ascension is the last of the risen Christ's appearances; and his true concern is with the Church's mission which continues the Christ event and will go on till he comes in glory.

NOTES

1. See U. Wilckens, *Die Auferstehung* (1970), E. T. *Resurrection* (The Saint Andrew Press, 1978).
2. See J. Jeremias, *Eucharistic Origins*, pp 101-103.
3. See V. Taylor, *The Formation of the Gospel Tradition*, chapter 3 and U. Wilckens, op. cit. pp 43-66.
4. The rabbis said: 'Sooner let the words of the Law be burnt than delivered to women.' 'Male chauvinists' we should call them nowadays.
5. H. Von Campenhausen, *Tradition and Life in the Church*, p 77. The story of the guard at the tomb (*Matthew* 27:62-66), peculiar to Matthew and probably 'secondary', implies that the grave was found empty, and that the Jews started the story of the stolen body to discredit the Christian claim. It shows that one fact was common to Jews and Christians in their debates: on the third day the body of Jesus was *not* to be found in the tomb.
6. In *Luke* 24:43 the risen Christ is said to have eaten broiled fish. This statement may have been meant to defend the disciples against the charge that what they had seen was a ghost. Yet, even in such stories, note that Jesus appears as someone who is in some sense already exalted, since he is one who can come through closed doors, appear and disappear (*Luke* 24:31; *John* 20:19). See G. B. Caird, *Saint Luke*, p 261, and compare *Luke* 3:22 'in bodily form'.
7. It has been made a count against the truth of the resurrection that those to whom Christ appeared were believers, not neutral witnesses. Believers they were *not*. So far from being buoyed up in faith, they were sunk in despair, and received the first tidings of Christ's victory 'as idle tales' (*Luke* 24:11). The truth is that those to whom Christ first appeared *became believers*. In their encounters with the risen Lord they were confronted, overwhelmed, and claimed by Christ.
8. *Colossians* 2:11f, 3:1ff is the fulfilment, in Christ, of Ezekiel's prophecy of Israel's resurrection from the dead, as Paul's language shows. See *Ezekiel* 37:1-14.
9. See John Baillie *And the Life Everlasting*, chapter 4.
10. *Sōma sēma*, said Plato, 'the body is a tomb'. For Paul, if *sarx* ('flesh') is man as doomed to perish, *sōma* ('body') is man as destined for God.
11. In his life of John Donne, Walton wrote of his hero, 'That body, which was once a temple of the Holy Ghost, is now become a small quantity of Christian dust. *But I shall see it reanimated*'.

Chapter 6

The Kingdom come with Power

I

Once, on the road to Jerusalem and the cross, Jesus prophesied, 'There are some of those standing here who will not taste death before they have seen the kingdom of God already come in power.' (*Mark* 9:1, *NEB*). He was not referring to what is known as his second advent.[1] The prophecy began to come true on the first Easter Day when he himself was 'appointed Son of God with power' (*Romans* 1:4) by the resurrection. It reached fulfilment seven weeks later, on the day of Pentecost when the Holy Spirit descended on the waiting disciples.[2] A poet has described the event:

When Christ had shown God's dawning Reign,
His Spirit came to lead,
That unto truth men might attain
And all the world be freed.

So, when with one accord combined,
The friends of Jesus came,
They heard God's Spirit like a wind,
They saw it like a flame.

And they who sat within the walls
With strange new ardour blazed,
Their voices rang like trumpet calls
And men thronged up amazed.[3]

Luke's description of the physical and psychical

phenomena is somewhat puzzling. The 'tongues as of fire' may have been like the fiery 'photisms' which men like Blaise Pascal and George Fox experienced in later Christian history. The Pentecostal 'gift of tongues' would seem to have been not some sudden expertise in foreign languages but that ecstatic speech under stress of strong religious emotion which later broke out at Corinth (*I Corinthians* 12-14) and has recurred often since in times of religious revival. Hence the bystanders' accusation (which Peter rebutted), 'These men have been drinking!' (*Acts* 2:13 *NEB*).

What is certain is that on this 'red-letter' day the Spirit came mightily on Jesus' followers so that, at last, Peter fulfilled the promise of his name, 'the rock-man'. But for them all Pentecost was the day of a *new* discovery, the discovery of a fellowship (*koinōnia*) with one another and with the risen Christ, unseen but not unknown, in their midst. Their discovery (which was indeed God's revelation) was that the era of the Holy Spirit had begun and the kingdom of God had come with power.

Few modern books on Christian doctrine accord the Holy Spirit the space given him in the writings of the apostles. Writing in 1931[4] to an Anglican friend, Principal David S Cairns of Aberdeen had this to say:

> What has grown on me of late years is the very great place the coming of the Spirit has in the apostolic writings. If you come to them with really fresh eyes, you cannot help seeing that they put an enormous importance on this as something new, a kind of 'wireless' between heaven and earth that was not there before. Because of this medium it was possible for every Christian church to be a kind of replica of the Galilean circle, with the living Christ still in the midst, messages continually coming and going. Nor do I think the impression conveyed is that these messages were confined, so to speak, to the governing hierarchy, but were regarded as a common possession, a permanent gift to every real community as such.

This is finely and truly said. As a result of the Pentecostal event, the risen Christ had become the *ubiquitous* Christ, 'let loose in the world where neither Roman nor Jew could stop his truth', and present 'wherever two or three were gathered together in his name'.

II

Here, however, we must pause to discuss the word 'spirit' in the Old Testament and the New.

The Hebrew word is *ruach*, the Greek *pneuma* (from which comes our word 'pneumatic'). Originally, both mean 'air in motion', be it 'wind' or 'breath'. Something in the physical world—the wind driving the desert sand before it, or the breath of a living creature—symbolises that incorporeal element in man which we call his 'spirit'. Then the word is applied to the supernatural power which man feels energising in him and which he believes to come from on high, from the unseen world of the divine. Thus the Holy Spirit is the wind, or breath, of the Almighty which operates in creation, works in history, and activates the life of man.

In the Old Testament the Holy Spirit mostly means the vital energy of the divine nature. It is God in action, God putting forth his power. So it is the source of Samson's strength when he slays a lion (*Judges* 14:6), of the prophets' inspiration (*I Samuel* 10:10), and of a clean heart (*Psalm* 51:10).

But in old Israel the Holy Spirit seems to work fitfully and individually, so that later prophets like Ezekiel and Joel look forward to a blessed time when God's Spirit will not only revivify the dead bones of God's people (*Ezekiel* 37:1-14) but will be outpoured 'on all flesh' (*Joel* 2:28-32: the passage quoted by Peter on the day of Pentecost).

III

If now we return to the New Testament, we find such prophecies in process of fulfilment, first in the work and words of Jesus the Messiah, and then in the New Israel on the first Whit Sunday.

In the gospels the Holy Spirit is at work in Jesus, first at his birth (*Matthew* 1:20; *Luke* 1:35) and afterwards in his ministry. On him, as he rises from his baptism, the Spirit descends to attest his divine sonship and equip him for his work (*Mark* 1:10f). In the Nazareth synagogue he cries, 'The Spirit of the Lord is upon me, because he has anointed me to preach the good news to the poor' (*Luke* 4:18f, quoting *Isaiah* 61:1f). By the Spirit's power he does his mighty works (*Matthew* 12:28, Q); and to ascribe them to the powers of darkness, as the scribes were doing, is (he says) to blaspheme against the Holy Spirit working in him (*Mark* 3:28f). In the memorable hours of his ministry, as the awareness of his unique divine sonship comes vividly home to him, he 'exults in the Holy Spirit' (*Luke* 10:21). So Jesus, the anointed of the Holy Spirit, lives and works under that Spirit's inspiration.

Yet, during his ministry, comments John, 'the Spirit was not yet, because Jesus was not yet glorified' (*John* 7:39). A puzzling remark till you realise that the Holy Spirit belongs essentially to the age of the Church. Though himself embodying the Spirit of God, Jesus could not bestow him on men till his earthly work was done and he himself risen and exalted to the right hand of his Father.

Nonetheless, as the ministry moves inexorably to its climax, we find Jesus promising his disciples that in days to come when they will stand trial before earthly rulers, they will have the Holy Spirit's help (*Mark* 13:11; *Luke* 12:12, Q). And at last in the upper room, with the cross

not far away, Jesus gives them explicit teaching about the
'Paraclete' who will be their Comforter, Remembrancer
and Advocate in the days beyond the cross (*John* 14:16-
18, 26; 15:26; 16:7-14). Then the Spirit who had been
incarnate in him, will indwell them also, acting as his *alter
ego*, or second self (not so much to supply his absence as
to accomplish his presence), and in their future work and
witness leading them into 'all the truth' (not 'truth' in the
wider modern sense as, e.g. 'the truth of science', but all
the truth about reality which Christ's coming involved)
and convicting the pagan world of its sinful unbelief.

IV

Now let us pass to the age of the apostles, or 'special
messengers', of Christ.

The book we call 'the *Acts*' serves as a bridge between
the four gospels and the rest of the New Testament. It tells
how, in three decades, the apostles carried the good news
about Jesus from Jerusalem to Rome. Yet the chief actor
in it is neither Peter nor Paul, large parts though they
played in the drama, but the Holy Spirit. It is the Spirit
who leads and empowers the young Church in its
outreach.

Luke's language about the Spirit is that of religious
experience rather than that of a systematic theologian.
Thus sometimes he describes the Spirit as an influence
that 'falls on' men and women. More often the Spirit acts
like a person, for he is said to prompt and guide the
councils of the Church in their deliberations and decision-
making. (cf. *Acts* 15:28: 'It seemed good to the Holy Spirit
and to us'.)

Once named 'the Spirit of Jesus' (16:7), he is ever the
Spirit of God bestowed by Christ, as he dynamically
directs the gospel's advance. First, he possesses Peter;

then Stephen, Philip, and Paul, sending them forth from Jerusalem to Samaria, from Samaria to Antioch, from Antioch to Greece, and finally from Greece to Rome, the world's capital. Fitly therefore has the *Acts of the Apostles* been named 'the Gospel of the Holy Spirit'.

Before we summarise what the apostles say about the Spirit, two points must be stressed.

First, if we think of the Spirit as some vague supernatural power, we are not on Christian ground. Always the Spirit is God's Spirit mediated by Christ so that we may say, 'The presence of the Spirit is Christ's own presence in spirit'.[5]

Second, 'faith' and 'Spirit' are correlative terms. That is to say, 'the Spirit' describes the Christian life as *divinely* determined, as the gift of God; whereas 'faith' describes the same life as *humanly* conditioned, a life which from first to last is one of trust in Christ.

Among the apostles it is not Peter, the ex-Galilean fisherman, but Paul, the trained theologian, who is the expositor *par excellence* of the Holy Spirit's nature and work. (The *loci classici* on the Spirit in his letters are *Romans* 8; *I Corinthians* 2, 12-14; *2 Corinthians* 3 and *Galatians* 5.)

How many and various are the roles which Paul assigns to the Spirit! He is liberator, illuminator, enabler, inspirer, interceder, bestower, uniter and assurer, all in one. The Holy Spirit liberates from the bonds of Jewish legalism, inspires men to confess Jesus as Lord, enables apostles to know 'the mind' ('purpose', almost 'theology') of Christ. The Spirit bestows all spiritual gifts (*charismata*: gifts of God's grace) of which the greatest is love (*agapé*). As the Spirit helps men to 'mortify' their lower natures and the power of sin in the flesh, so he binds men into Christian fellowship (*koinōnia*). He it is who aids Christians in their prayers, as he 'causes all things to work together for their good'. By the same Spirit they are moved to cry 'Abba, Father', and love, joy and peace, with 'all the virtues we possess', are the Spirit's gracious fruits in Christian living. By the Holy Spirit God took Christ out of the grave. So the same Spirit, indwelling believers in him, is 'the down-payment and guarantee' (*arrabōn*) of the glory God has in store for those who love him.

If we turn to that other 'prince among the apostles', Peter, we find him writing of his readers' 'hallowing by the Holy Spirit' (*I Peter* 1:2, doubtless a reference to their reception of the Spirit at baptism). The Church he describes as a 'spiritual house' (*I Peter* 2:4f) composed of 'living stones', i.e. Spirit-filled Christians. And he assures his readers threatened with persecution that 'the Holy Spirit sent from heaven' (*I Peter* 1:12) 'is resting on them' (4:14).

John, like Paul, finds possession by the Holy Spirit proof of Christ's indwelling in the believer (*I John* 3:24). The test for distinguishing this Spirit from all false ones is the confession that Jesus Christ has come in the flesh, i.e. an acknowledgement of his true humanity (*I John* 4:2). As for his divinity, together with 'the water' (his baptism) and 'the blood' (his atoning death), the Spirit attests Jesus as God's Son (*I John* 5:6).

According to the writer of *Hebrews*, the salvation proclaimed by Christ has been confirmed by 'gifts of the Holy Spirit' (2:4). Christians are described as those who 'have tasted the heavenly gift and shared in the Holy Spirit' (6:4); and to go back on one's Christian profession is to 'spurn the Son of God' who died for them and 'outrage God's gracious Spirit' (10:29).

Finally, it was when John, the seer of Patmos, was 'in the Spirit on the Lord's Day' (*Revelation* 1:10) that he was granted his tremendous visions of the judgment and victory of God and the glories of 'Jerusalem the Golden'. 'Hear what the Spirit says to the churches!', he commands the Christians in Ephesus (*Revelation* 2:7). And his book ends with the evangelical summons of the Church to the world, 'And the Spirit and the Bride say, "Come!"' (*Revelation* 22:17).

Thus, to sum up, it is by the Pentecostal gift of the Holy Spirit that the risen and exalted Lord still carries on his work on earth; he is now present with us through the Holy Spirit; and in the work of that Spirit the ends are secured for which Christ lived and died and rose again.

Such is the New Testament's teaching. No wonder then that the early Christians could not express all that they meant by the word 'God' till they had said 'Father, Son and Holy Spirit' (*Matthew* 28:19; *2 Corinthians* 1:21f, 13:14; *Ephesians* 2:18; *I Peter* 1:2; *Jude* 20f). Here is 'the Trinity of experience', as it has been called, from which the later Church doctrine of the triune God was to grow.

So 'the apostolic Church worshipped one God in Trinity and Trinity in unity. The one true God of the old Jewish faith, the God of Abraham, Isaac and Jacob, had now acted in a new way: what was involved was not an enlargement of God, but an enlargement of man's revealed knowledge of God, not the taking of two other 'persons' into the divine society, but the revelation of God's different ways of being God.'[6]

V

Such was the Spirit of God in the glad springtime of the faith when, as one loving heart set another aflame, the gospel (in Carlyle's phrase) 'flew like hallowed fire from soul to soul' and brought new life and light and hope to 'that hard pagan world' of the first century AD. How fares it today with 'the Lord and Giver of Life' (as the Nicene Creed names him)?

If an unprejudiced outsider were to make a report on many sections of western Christendom today, might he not conclude that many Christians were not unlike those disciples Paul met at Ephesus who 'had not even heard that there was a Holy Spirit' (*Acts* 19:1ff)? Or perhaps like the modern minister's son who said, 'Dad, I can understand you when you say that you believe in God the Father and in Jesus Christ his Son, but when you say that you believe in the Holy Ghost, I haven't a clue'.

In many parts of the world (and especially where belief in the Holy Spirit is paramount) the gospel *is* making spectacular progress.[7] But no honest observer of the European scene can deny that much of the *Geist* (German for 'spirit') has gone out of its Christianity.

How has this come about? Doubtless the loss of *Geist* is due to the influence of what the Germans call the *Zeitgeist*, 'the spirit of the age'. Secularised and science-minded modern man has his doubts about anything which smacks of the supernatural, as the Holy Spirit certainly does. Accordingly, in the nineteen-forties, Rudolph Bultmann declared belief in spirits to be impossible for men accustomed to use electricity and the wireless.[8] Such first-century 'myths', he said, must be re-interpreted in terms of modern existential philosophy, if the gospel were to come home to men today. So, whereas Paul had filled his pages with references to the Holy Spirit, Bultmann peppered his with the existentialists' favourite word, 'decision' (*Entscheidung*).

Bultmann was mistaken. It is no harder to believe in the Holy Spirit after the invention of electric light than before. Rightly did Stephen Neil[9] describe Bultmann's theology as 'a gallant attempt to make the challenge of the gospel relevant to modern man without a doctrine of the Holy Spirit.'

Nor are our British *Honest to God* theologians very different. When someone asked Barth what he thought of their 'new theology', he replied: 'When I am in an irenic mood, I say this is flat-tyre theology. The *pneuma* (which is Greek for 'air' and 'spirit') has gone out of it; and when the *pneuma* goes out of a tyre, the automobile is likely to have an accident.'[10]

So much for the dark side of the modern picture. Happily, it is far from the whole story. Signs of hope for better things, of worthier Christian thinking about the Holy Spirit, have already appeared on the horizon.

In the first chapter of the Bible the Spirit of God is connected with his work of creation—'And the Spirit of God moved upon the face of the waters'—and if, as we must believe, *ultimate reality* is all of a piece, then revealed theology must be capable of being reconciled with natural theology, and the Spirit which worked and works still in creation (Cf *John* 5:17, 'My Father has never yet ceased his work, and I am working too') must be one and the same as the Spirit bestowed by the exalted Christ.

This was the task to which, in our times, Charles Raven and Teilhard de Chardin set their hands. Their purpose was to show that the Holy Spirit's work was to be traced in the creative as well as the inspirational energies of the Godhead, and so formulate a Christ-centred view of the universe which would heal the breach between science and Christianity.

Yet perhaps the most suggestive modern book on this subject has been Bishop J. V. Taylor's *The Go-between God* where the Spirit is conceived as at once opening our eyes to God's glories in creation and his grace in Christ. Starting from a natural theology of the Spirit, he writes refreshingly of the Holy Spirit as 'the Anonymous Third Party' or 'Medium in our midst' who unseals our vision to God's living presence in his world and enables us also to see his glory in the face of Christ (*2 Corinthians* 4:6).

He then turns to discuss the Pentecostal movement which, originating at the beginning of this century among American negroes, has now spread to all the churches.

The Pentecostals claim to have re-discovered the power which came upon Christ's first followers at Pentecost. Whatever we think of them—and some of us deprecate their obsession with 'tongues' and have our doubts about their doctrine of 'the second blessing'[11]—none may deny that Pentecostalism is the fastest growing movement in Christianity today, that it registers a needed protest against an overly 'cerebral' Christianity, and that it has revitalised many moribund congregations.

VI

Let us draw our study to a practical conclusion. As we understand the historic revelation of God in Christ, there is nothing in it which may not recur, and is not meant of God to recur. Does not this hold true of that 'wireless between heaven and earth' which fills the *Book of Acts* and the apostolic letters? God's gift in Christ of the Holy Spirit has not been withdrawn; and if the Church today is not living on the ancient levels, it is because Christians, for one reason or another, do not appropriate this gift, or fail to recognise how the Spirit often works and therefore (as the phrase goes) do not give honour where honour is due.

For the Spirit can come not only in the excitement of a revivalist convention but in the quiet of a Quaker meeting. He can come as he did to John on the lonely isle of Patmos, or in a Bedford jail as he did to Bunyan. He can come as the 'Comforter', i.e. strengthener, in times of bereavement when, as many have testified, they 'get strength' to bear their bitter loss. He can come as we study the words of prophet or evangelist, so that the Bible becomes a sacramental book, able to speak its Word of God to us today.

So our fathers and forefathers found by experience. Is it because in the hurly-burly of this twentieth century we can find no time for such quiet waiting upon God that we have earned for ourselves the nickname of 'God's frozen people'? Criticise them as we will, may we not learn from our Pentecostalist brethren for whom the Spirit has become a dynamic and present reality? And when John Mackay[12] of Princeton writes, 'If it is a choice between the uncouth life of the Pentecostals and the aesthetic death of the older churches, I for one choose life', many of us find an answering echo in our own hearts. For have they not recovered much of that spiritual fervour, that holy enthusiasm, which moved the young Church in the first century to go forth conquering and to conquer?

In his book *Enthusiasm* Monsignor Ronald Knox quoted an imaginary conversation between Erasmus, the great Renaissance humanist, and a brother named Trophimus. Said Trophimus: 'Inertia is the only vice, Master Erasmus, and the only virtue is . . .' 'What?' broke in Erasmus. 'Why enthusiasm!' came the answer. 'And', comments Dr William Lillie[13] (to whom I owe the reference) 'enthusiasm is the essential quality of the Holy Spirit and of Spirit-filled men.'

In this we seem to hear an echo of Paul writing to the Romans: 'Never flag in zeal, be aglow with the Spirit, serve the Lord' (*Romans* 12:11), and pointing us today to the secret of renewal in Christ's Church. Is it not high time for us 'dis-Spirited' Christians to hark back to the apostolic source of life and power and, in our work and witness, expose ourselves afresh to

> ... that Breath
> Of God in man that warranteth
> The utmost, inmost things of faith[14]?

This is the doctrine of a dynamic God. This is the doctrine that many of us need to hear, as our prayer should be:

> Breathe on us, Breath of God,
> Fill us with life anew!

NOTES

1. See G. B. Caird's essay in *Biblical Studies* (Essays in honour of William Barclay), pp 74ff.
2. According to *John* 20:22, the risen Christ gave the Spirit to his disciples on the first Easter evening, breathing on them with the words 'Receive the Holy Spirit'. Is this irreconcilable with *Acts* 2? Is it not indeed psychologically probable that there should have been a period of waiting while the Spirit worked among the disciples, like yeast in dough, till it burst forth at Pentecost in a mighty release of divine power?
3. *Songs of Praise,* p 185.
4. David Cairns, *An Autobiography*, p 200.
5. Cf *Romans* 8:9f, where God's Spirit = Christ's Spirit = 'Christ in you'.
6. A. Richardson, *Introduction to the Theology of the New Testament*, p 122.
7. According to MARCO, an American institute for missionary research, the worldwide Church every day is gaining fifty-five thousand new converts, as every week sees the establishment of fourteen hundred new churches.
8. *Kerygma and Myth*, p 5.

9. *The Interpretation of the New Testament, 1861-1961*, p 233.

10. *How I changed my Mind*, p 83.

11. What do the Pentecostals mean by 'the second blessing'? As we understand them, there must be after conversion and 'water baptism' a 'baptism in the Spirit' like that which Christ's followers received at Pentecost. Mediated by the laying on of hands, it should be accompanied by 'tongues' ('no tongues, no baptism in the Spirit'). The recipient of this 'second blessing' is henceforward expected not only to witness for Christ but, when necessary, to perform miracles, e.g. of healing. See S. T. Tugwell, *Did you receive the Spirit?*, chapter 5. Tugwell, a Dominican priest, argues that Pentecostalism is in harmony both with the Bible and with Roman Catholic theology.

12. W. Hollenweger, *The Pentecostals*, p 6.

13. *A Confession of Faith*, pp 46f.

14. D. G. Rossetti in his poem 'The World's Worth'.

Chapter 7

The Last Things

We have seen that the kingdom of God was initiated in Christ's work and words, and that it came 'with power' by the resurrection and the advent of the Spirit. But the men of the New Testament also look forward to a future climax of the kingdom when their Lord will come in glory and God will complete the saving work he began in Christ.

Thus we have the paradox that the age to come is at once a present experience and a future consummation, so that the Christian's life is marked by a tension between what has already happened and what will happen, between this world where we have seen 'the light of the knowledge of the glory of God in the face of Christ' (2 *Corinthians* 4:6) and a world to come in which all the promises of God in Christ will come fully true and his kingdom will be consummated.

All this belongs to what the theologians call eschatology, the doctrine of the Last Things, i.e. death, judgment, heaven and hell. Before we discuss them, it will be well to summarise the situation today.

I

Time was when Christian divines dwelt much on the Last Things. Those who know Hamish Hendry's poem 'The Beadle's Lament'[1] will recall how this Scottish 'minister's man' deplored the replacement of his old hell-fire preaching pastor by the 'modernist' young one with his God 'wha widna fricht the craws':

A kind o' thowless Great First Cause
Skinklin through vapour.

Now, except perhaps in some 'fundamentalist' circles the old-time 'sanctions' (i.e. condign penalties hereafter for non-observance of God's laws) have largely gone, so that for many Christians the word 'eschatology' has come to mean little more than the question, 'If a man die, shall he live again?' Thus have 'the acids of modernity' bitten into the things once most surely believed.

Yet, paradoxically enough, if the modern Christian has jettisoned much of his forefathers' eschatology, secularised man today cannot apparently get along without some other sort of eschatology. If religion fails to furnish him with a credible other-worldly hope, he will quickly find secular substitutes for it, like Hitler's dream of a *Reich* that would last a thousand years, or the Marxist myth of a classless society to supervene upon the final 'show-down' between communism and capitalism.

Moreover, in this century the belief in progress, born of nineteenth century evolutionary doctrine, has suffered grave if not fatal damage. Up until 1914 it provided many thinking people with a working philosophy of history. Man, it was believed, was out of the woods at last and marching to perfection. Since then, two world catastrophes and their awful aftermaths have made most of them take a much less sanguine view of human progress, and with the invention of the H-bomb and the threat of nuclear holocaust the end of the world as we know it has become a live possibility.

The time would appear to be ripe then for the Christian

Church to begin re-thinking its beliefs about the Last Things. For if Christianity is true—if God was really in Christ—then the kingdom which he proclaimed, embodied, and inaugurated must have a consummation. Belief in eschatology without belief in such a consummation would be like belief in religion without belief in God.

Where then do we start? What is the right approach to a Christian doctrine of the last things?

II

Christianity, it will be agreed, offers man three things: a unique self-disclosure of God in Christ, a new way of life, and an immortal hope. And the first thing to be said is that *any modern doctrine of the Last Things must be based on the revelation of God's nature and purpose which we already have in Christ.*

Modern man may doubt whether Christian theology builds on anything more than the speculations of faith. In this he is mistaken. As Alan Richardson showed in his *Christian Apologetics*, Christian theology is an empirical science using the same methods as other inductive sciences such as physics or biology. Its distinctive *datum* is the historical self-revelation of God in Christ; it deals with indubitable facts of human experience, namely, a community of faith owing its existence to a series of events in history regarded as acts of the living God; and its task is to formulate doctrines of the End consonant with the revelation given to faith in the present. Our statements about the last things are therefore not mere pious guess-work, as some suppose, but 'transpositions into the key of the hereafter' of that knowledge of God which we already have in our encounter with God in Christ.

This was Paul's view in the greatest chapter he ever wrote. 'What then shall we say to these things?' he asked, after his masterly exposition of God's grace in Christ to sinners, 'If God is for us, who can be against us? He who did not spare his own Son but gave him up for us all, how shall he not with him freely give us all things? . . . For I am persuaded that neither death nor life . . . shall be able to separate us from the love of God in Christ Jesus our Lord.' (*Romans* 8:31-39).

Here Christian faith in a blessed life hereafter is an *inference* from the doctrine of our redemption. The God who cared, and cares, for us (says Paul) will care for us forever—till beyond all danger, darkness, and death we shall see him 'face to face' (*I Corinthians* 13:12).

The second point is that today *we cannot accept all our forefathers' beliefs about the last things*. We live in a scientific age; and modern science, not least biblical science, has had a purgative effect on our Christian thinking.

It is not only that since Copernicus, Darwin and Einstein our whole world-view has been revolutionised but that, thanks to biblical criticism (which, when wisely used, can be an instrument of the Holy Spirit to lead us into gospel truth), we have rejected some of our forefathers' personal notions about the Last Things. To take only two examples. First, how many Christians today would avow their faith in a God, like that of Burns's 'Holy Willie', who predestines

> . . . one to heaven and ten to hell,
> all for his glory?

Or how many Christians nowadays believe, as our forefathers did (in spite of *I Corinthians* 15:50), in a re-animation of corpses at the last day?

On the other hand, what we share with our Christian

forefathers (as with the apostles) is the conviction that
Christ is the centre of history, that in him God was
reconciling the world to himself, that in the cross and
resurrection and the advent of the Holy Spirit the End has
begun, and that we 'live between the times'—the time
when God broke decisively into history to redeem his
people and the time when he will consummate his saving
rule in the glories of another world.

<h1 style="text-align:center">III</h1>

Let us therefore consider the consummation of that
kingdom, often in the New Testament named the
parousia, or royal coming, of Christ and traditionally his
'second advent'.

A study of Christ's sayings about the future[2] shows
that, besides predicting his own triumph over death and
exaltation to God's presence (*Mark* 9:31, 14:62), he also
envisaged a future glorious coming. This is what the early
Christians had in mind when they prayed '*Marana tha*'
('Our Lord, come!') (*I Corinthians* 16:22; *Revelation*
22:20). But two things are to be noted about his teaching.
First, he himself did not know 'the day or the hour' (*Mark*
13:32). And, second, to judge from his own words, he did
not conceive it as a coming *in* history. For an event which
presupposes the breakdown of the physical universe
(*Mark* 13:24-27) and gathers together all the generations
of men who have ever lived (*Matthew* 25:31-46), must lie
outside the order of space and time as we know it.[3]

Down the centuries Christians have often taken to predicting the visible return of Christ to earth only, when the
day or year came and went, to find their hope unfulfilled.
It may be reverently suggested that theirs was a two-fold
error: first, in conceiving his coming as an event in history

and, second, in thinking of it in terms of human clock-time when in Christ's view it was a matter of God's time.

Yet their spiritual instinct was not wrong. Christians cannot dispense with the truth for which the second advent stands, namely, that the Creator, who is the Father of Christ, must finally cry, 'It is finished!' to the work he took in hand when he sent his Son into the world. Belief in eschatology without belief in such an End would be like belief in religion without belief in God.

The hope of Christ's royal coming expresses our faith that history must have a consummating close. It is not just going on for ever—that would be endlessly boring. Neither do we believe, as the Greeks did, that it is simply going round in circles. That would be hopeless and Godless. It is our belief that history will end in a climax when God will complete his saving work and his Son will be revealed in his true glory. Then the hiddenness of his Easter victory will be disclosed (*Colossians* 3:4).

Yet, if we cannot jettison such a hope, it is a hope directed to a consummation beyond history. Such, we believe, was Christ's own view. But there is a further consideration. To regard his glorious advent as merely an event *in* time would be to turn the ultimate victory of God *over* time, which is what the consummation of his kingdom means—into a mere event *in* time.[4]

The second advent is the point at which history—and all in it well-pleasing to God—will be taken up into his eternity. It is the climax at which the human race will reach its last frontier post and come face to face with God in Christ. Of course such an event passes all our imagining. But in one respect it will be like his first coming, for we shall encounter the same person whose grace and goodness are already known to us from the gospel pages; and if we have to stand before him at a last judgment

D

(whatever form it take), we may believe that the sign of the cross will be over all.

IV

So to the traditional alternatives of human destiny, heaven and hell, and the question of who goes where:

What the New Testament means by 'heaven', or 'paradise',[5] we shall consider presently. Enough now to say that it means being in the presence of God and his Son in that state of pure blessedness promised in the beatitudes. But what are we to say about 'hell' in days like these when it has become a meaningless expletive on the lips of men?

Modern Christians have rightly repudiated the horrendous hell-fire preaching of earlier centuries, because it is impossible to reconcile with Christ's teaching about a heavenly Father who is 'kind to the ungrateful and the wicked' (*Luke* 6:35) and whose 'goodness knows no bounds' (*Matthew* 5:48, *NEB*), and also because most of the terrible texts about 'eternal punishment', 'gnashing of teeth' and 'everlasting fire' come from Matthew's gospel and are rightly judged, even by conservative modern scholars like Jeremias, to be 'secondary', i.e. attributable not to Jesus but to the evangelist.

Nevertheless, Christ did solemnly warn men of the peril of unrepented sin, of the state of mind that deliberately calls good evil, and of the possibility of 'perdition'. For him, 'going to hell' was the opposite of 'entering into life'. It meant eternal exclusion from God's presence. Long ago John Donne wrote: 'When all is done, the hell of hells, the torment of torments, is the everlasting absence of God, and the everlasting impossibility of returning to his presence.'[6] And this, agrees a modern theologian like

Wolfhart Pannenberg[7], is the one decisive factor, or feature, in a valid concept of hell. In other words, the only fit and proper punishment for incorrigible wickedness is not (in Dean Inge's phrase) 'to be cooked in an oven', or tortured in eternal flame, but to become quite incapable, here or hereafter, of seeing the God who has made us for himself.

But if our Lord does allow for the possibility of men 'perishing', it is not our business to deny it or to try 'to people' hell. It is the egotism of men which has led them to speculate about the eternal fate of others. When Christ himself was asked if only a few were to be saved, he turned the question of theological curiosity into one of existential decision. 'Few enough', he answered in effect, 'to make you fear you may not be there. See to your own entry!' (*Luke* 13:23f). What we may believe is that the God and Father of Christ will not permit the sentence to fall on any who do not deliberately pronounce it on themselves.

V

We come, lastly, to consider what Peter describes as the 'inheritance, imperishable, undefiled and unfading, kept in heaven for you.' (*I Peter* 1:4).

Here the first thing to be said is that we should heed John's warning: 'It does not yet appear what we shall be' (*I John* 3:2). The reserve which John exercises should be ours also. Thus, as Reinhold Niebuhr said, it is no part of Christian wisdom to presume a detailed knowledge of either the furniture of heaven or the temperature of hell. Nevertheless, the New Testament revelation entitles us to make three affirmations:

First, *Christian immortality is the gift of God and is bound up with the risen Christ*, 'Christ in us the hope of

glory' (*Colossians* 1:27). 'Because I live, you will **live**
also', promises the Christ of John (*John* 14:19), a promise
given vibrant expression in Sydney Carter's 'Lord of the
Dance':

> They buried my body,
> And they thought I'd gone,
> But I am the Dance
> And I still go on.
>
> They cut me down,
> But I leapt up high;
> I am the life
> That'll never die.
> I'll live in you,
> If you'll live in me,
> For I am the Lord of the Dance, said he.

Second, *Christian hope is centred not in the survival of the
soul but in the resurrection of the body, i.e. of the whole
man.* Here the classic exposition is *I Corinthians* 15.
What does Paul teach? We are not immortal in our
own right. 'In Adam all die.' Death is a real end. If man is
to live again, only the living God can give him new life.
And this is his promise in Christ (*I Corinthians* 15:49).

It is the promise that hereafter God will give us a new
medium of self-expression, a spiritual body or organism,
i.e. a 'body' suited to the conditions of the next world as
our present body of flesh is to the conditions of this one.
Yet, equally, this future 'body' will re-affirm our present
identity. 'If I am a somebody now—an individual with a
name—then, by God's goodness, I shall be the samebody
then.'[8] 'I find this doctrine most comforting and re-
assuring', writes Dr William Lillie, 'It speaks not of the
poor done body which will soon be earth, but of the whole

personality (and not an abstracted soul) being expressed in a body of a new kind.'[9]

Third, *the other life then is the other life now*. Eternity does not lie merely at the end of time. It pervades it now, 'beats at our own clay-shuttered doors', and every genuine Christian experience in this life is a sample in advance of the heavenly life. This is what John means when he talks of 'eternal life' as a present possession, as likewise Paul when he calls the Holy Spirit an *arrabōn,* that is, a first instalment-cum-guarantee of glory to come (*2 Corinthians* 5:5; *Ephesians* 1:14).

From this it follows that what matters is not the moment of bodily death but the time when a man comes to be 'in Christ'. Life hereafter will not be a completely new life but rather that which he already has in his faith-union with Christ, only it will be lived under other and unimaginably more glorious conditions. The present relation of being 'in Christ' will have given place to that of being 'with Christ' in the heavenly places, and our present 'lowly' bodies will have become like Christ's 'body of glory' (*Philippians* 3:21).

Rightly is the New Testament reticent about life in heaven, since we are here concerned with what 'eye has not seen nor ear heard', and we may therefore speak of it only in symbols, such symbols as the seer of Patmos uses when he seeks to describe 'Jerusalem the Golden' (*Revelation* 21:1-22:5).

Yet on two points the New Testament lays stress. First, we pass into no lone immortality. Life hereafter will be corporate—a life of fellowship with God our Father in the presence of his Son and all the redeemed (*Revelation* 7:9-17). 'The life supernal', if we may so name it, will be a great society of redeemed persons living for ever with their Lord in a communion no longer hampered by the flesh, no longer at the mercy of death; for 'this corruptible will have put on incorruption', and Christ's people will be at home in their Father's house in a beatitude beyond all conceiving.

Second, 'we shall be like him, for we shall see him as he is' (*I John* 3:2). Nothing less than Christ-likeness is our final destiny, for it is our heavenly Father's purpose that we should be 'shaped to the likeness of his Son' (*Romans* 8:29, *NEB*). 'Every Christian', wrote C. S. Lewis,[10] 'is to become a little Christ'.

With such a hope in prospect we ought then to labour in the Lord unwearyingly (*I Corinthians* 15:58), knowing that our work is 'not in vain'. Communist jibes about 'pie in the sky when you die' should not worry us unduly. Our Christian hope is no 'opiate of the people' but a spiritual inheritance challenging us to yet more strenuous Christian endeavour in this life: 'a hope so great and so divine' as to beget in us 'immortal longings' and to give human life a meaning and an end which so many today need more than anything else to assure them that life is worth living and that Christ crucified, risen and regnant is God's master-key to its mystery.

Well might the Christian man or woman facing death make his own the words which, near the end of *The Pilgrim's Progress*, Mr Standfast uses to describe his own situation: 'I see myself now at the end of my journey, my toilsome days are ended. I have formerly lived by Hearsay and faith; but now I go where I shall live by sight, and shall be with Him in whose company I delight.'

NOTES

1. See John Buchan's *The Northern Muse*, pp 230-34.
2. See the author's *Work and Words of Jesus*, chapter 12.

3. On this whole subject see C. H. Dodd's *The Coming of Christ* (1951); T. F. Glasson's *The Second Advent* (3rd and revised edition, 1963); J. A. T. Robinson, *Jesus and his Coming* (1957); G. E. Ladd, *Jesus and the Kingdom* (1966).

4. See R. Niebuhr, *The Nature and Destiny of Man*.

5. Jesus' word to the penitent thief (*Luke* 23:43) is best taken as a striking application of the doctrine of justification by faith rather than as a metaphysical statement about the condition of the departed.

6. *Eighty Sermons*, p 776.

7. *Jesus God and man*, pp 270f.

8. C. F. D. Moule, *Christianity Revalued*, p 69.

9. *A Confession of Faith*, p 39.

10. *Beyond Personality*, p 28.

Chapter 8

The Person of Christ

What is the truth about Jesus Christ? How are we to explain One who dominates the New Testament, has inspired the lives of countless Christians, and whose power, 'deep in the general heart of man', survives to this very day, invading 'show business', television and even hippy sub-cultures? Is he simply a man like the rest of us (though incomparably better)? Is he superman? Or is he the God-man, our man from heaven?

This is the question, as the evidence to be examined is three-fold:

(1) The claim of Jesus himself.
(2) The testimony of his apostles.
(3) The voice of Christian experience.

I

Begin with the gospels. Did Jesus regard himself simply as the prophet of God's inbreaking kingdom, or did he believe himself to be central to it?

As we have seen, the kingdom of God in the gospels means God in his sovereign grace invading history in order to save his people from their sins and woes. Now you cannot study the gospels perceptively without noting that Jesus appears and acts as the living embodiment of his own great gospel. Where he is, the kingdom is—God acting. To be discipled to him is to be 'in the kingdom', in the realm of God's salvation. So we find a great twentieth century theologian like Karl Barth concurring with Marcion in the 2nd century AD that 'in the gospel the kingdom of God is Christ himself' (*in evangelio est regnum Dei Christus ipse*). Near the end of his life, in a TV interview, Barth was asked, 'Has your view of Christ changed over the years?' 'Yes', replied the honest old man, 'At the beginning I thought Christ was the prophet of the kingdom of God. Now I know that he *is* the Kingdom.' So Barth 'changed his mind' and with good warrant from the sayings of Jesus himself.

To begin with, his parables often contain 'implicit Christology', veiled hints of who Christ knew himself to be; little hints, for example, like that of the Stronger Man (*Luke* 11:21f) or the Apprenticed Son (*John* 5:19f); or longer ones like the Two Builders (*Matthew* 7:24-27) and the Last Judgment (*Matthew* 25:31-46) where Jesus poises the whole future of man on the response they make to his words, or their concern for 'the least of these his brethren'.

Many of the parables in fact were 'weapons of war' and means whereby his strategy was vindicated until no further words could avail but only an act—the deed of the cross. Especially is this true of those parables of crisis which he spoke as his ministry moved to its climax in Jerusalem. One thinks of the Barren Fig Tree (*Luke* 13:6-9), the Man on his way to Court (*Luke* 12:57-59), the Ten Bridesmaids (*Matthew* 25:1-13), the Traveller at Sunset (*John* 12:35f), the Wicked Vinedressers (*Mark* 12:1-9) and the Grain of Wheat which must die if it is to bear fruit (*John* 12:24).

Here, if we have ears to hear, Jesus is saying things which none short of the Messiah had the right to say, and knowing himself to be the sole bearer of Israel's destiny and the initiator of the new age. 'The grief Jesus carries', it has been finely said, 'is that of the sole burden-bearer, the

lone doer of God's perfect will. On the cross he is himself
Israel—Israel as God determined it, the vicarious bearer
of human destiny and hope no less than of human sin and
suffering. The old Israel dies in him, and in the very same
moment the new Israel is born.'[1]

To this evidence must now be added the 'I-sayings',
those utterances of Jesus dominated by the first personal
pronoun ('I'). Think of the 'I' in his saying 'If *I* by the
finger of God cast out devils, then is the kingdom of God
come upon you (*Luke* 11:20); or the 'I' in his great invita-
tion, 'Come unto me, and *I* will give you rest' (*Matthew*
11:28) or the sovereign 'I' which sounds six times through
the Sermon on the Mount: 'But *I* say unto you' (*Matthew*
5:21-48).

Similar are his 'I came' sayings: 'I came not to destroy
but to fulfil' (*Matthew* 5:17); 'I came not to call the righteous but sinners' (*Mark* 2:17); 'I came not to bring peace
but a sword' (*Matthew* 10:34); 'I came to send fire on the
earth' (*Luke* 12:49). Such sayings attest a mission to men
which moves us to ask, 'Who then is this who knows
himself so sent, so authorised, by God?

Lastly, recall those numerous sayings (some seventy-
four in all) which begin, 'Amen I tell you'. When we use
the word 'Amen', like the Jews, it means 'So be it!' at the
end of prayer or reading of holy writ. Not so did Jesus use
it. With the formula 'Amen I tell you' he prefaced many
sayings about the kingdom. To this style of speech there is
no parallel. Jesus said, 'Amen I tell you' and no other
man—not even a prophet—ever did. 'Amen I tell you,
whoever does not receive the kingdom of God as a little
child shall not enter it' (*Mark* 10:15). 'Amen I tell you,
there are some standing here who will not taste death till
they see the kingdom of God come with power' (*Mark*
9:1). 'Amen I tell you, as you did it to one of the least of

these my brothers, you did it unto me' (*Matthew* 25:40); and so on.

What is the source of this unique way of speaking? It is his awareness of being the Messiah, the bearer of God's saving rule to men. When he thus prefaces a saying, he implies that it is not his own but God's, that he but passes on what he has received from on high.

On any other lips but his such 'I' language would be deemed 'egoism', an unhealthy obsession with self. Egoist Christ was, but his egoism was for others' sake and the cause of the Kingdom which took him finally to the cross.[2]

Two more stones must be added to the cairn of proof connecting the person of Jesus with the kingdom of the Father.

First, the great thanksgiving (*Matthew* 11:25f, Q). In these verses[3] Jesus claims to be the Son of God in a lonely and unshared sense, and the sole mediator of his unique knowledge of God as Father to men: 'I thank thee, Father, Lord of heaven and earth, that thou hast hidden these things from the wise and understanding and revealed them to babes: yea, Father, for such was thy gracious will. All things have been delivered to me by my Father; and no one knows the Son except the Father; and no one knows the Father except the Son, and anyone to whom the Son chooses to reveal him.'

Yet perhaps his most remarkable self-revelation Jesus kept for the upper room. 'This is my body'—his word over the broken bread—is remarkable enough. Even more so his word over the cup, with the red Passover wine gleaming in it, 'This cup is the new covenant in my blood' (*I Corinthians* 11:25; *Mark* 14:24).

Centuries earlier, at the very nadir of old Israel's fortunes, the prophet Jeremiah had seen their only hope of salvation in God's making with them 'a new covenant', a new religious relation between God and men, carrying with it, as its fundamental blessing, the forgiveness of sins (*Jeremiah* 31:31ff). When Jesus speaks to the Twelve in the upper room, it is as if he were pointing to that prophecy and saying, 'Today is this scripture being fulfilled before your very eyes'. Then who is this who knows that by his sacrificial death he will inaugurate this new and blessed 'covenant' between God and men?

The conclusion is inescapable. *Jesus was quite central to the gospel of God's kingdom which he proclaimed.*

King Louis XIV of France once told his parliament, 'I am the state' (*l'état c'est moi*). No such swelling claim to earthly power and glory is to be found on our Lord's lips; yet in his earthly ministry, his work as the Servant-Messiah, he was the saving rule of his Father, incarnate and in action.

Before we turn to the apostles' teaching, let us recall what was said earlier about the connection between the kingdom, the cross and the resurrection. Since the kingdom was initiated in Jesus' ministry, we may not say that he died to bring it in. The cross falls within the framework of the kingdom, represents its burning focus and climax, is the crowning deed in God's holy warfare against the powers of evil, the condition not of the kingdom's coming but of its coming 'with power': its effectuation.

On the sacrifice of the cross God set his seal by raising his Son from the dead. The resurrection was God's vindication of the 'work' which Jesus 'finished' at Calvary.

II

In the letters of the apostles, for the most part, the place of the kingdom of God has been taken by Christ himself. But, if we reflect on the matter, this should not surprise us.

Why? Because by his death and resurrection Christ became all that the kingdom had contained. The Galilean gospel of the kingdom was Christ in essence; Christ crucified and risen is the kingdom come in power. He is the truth of his own greatest gospel. And this is why we must never think our study of Christ ended with the gospels. 'It needs the whole of the New Testament to show who Christ is', said James Denney, and he was right.

What then is the place of the apostles in the economy of revelation, i.e. God's self-disclosure in Christ? Of course the apostles bore their testimony to what they knew of Christ incarnate, crucified and risen. Listen to John, for example:

'That which was from the beginning, which we have heard, which we have seen with our own eyes, which we have looked upon and touched with our hands, concerning the word of life—the life was made manifest, and we saw it, and testify to it.' (*I John* 1:1f).

But never did they think of themselves as religious geniuses indoctrinating their readers with their own private speculations about Christ. They knew themselves to be *agents of the Holy Spirit*.

To discover how they regard their teaching, turn to *I Corinthians* 2[4] where Paul speaks not for himself only but for the apostles generally. What the apostles have to teach they regard as the authentic teaching of the risen Lord mediated to them through Christ's *alter ego*, the Holy Spirit, so that they dare to claim, 'We have the mind of Christ' (*I Corinthians* 2:16) or, as Moffatt renders it, 'Our thoughts are the thoughts of Christ.'

Thus, through his apostles, Christ interpreted his *finished* work as truly as in his passion sayings (about 'cup' 'baptism' and 'ransom') he interpreted his *unfinished* work.

We cannot here discuss in detail the apostles' Spirit-given teaching about Christ or the tremendous titles they apply to him. Led by the Spirit, they are wrestling with the questions, 'What are we to say of the Christ who has done this great and God-like thing for us?' 'What name or category best fits this man in whom God has inaugurated his new age and brought deliverance from sin and death?' 'Messiah, Lord, Son of God, the Word made flesh?' Yet, however much these titles of majesty vary, through them runs one basic concept of Christ's person. Whether it is Paul, John, Peter, the Writer to the Hebrews, or the Seer of Patmos, of two things they are convinced. One is that Christ was true man, 'bone of our bone, and flesh of our flesh'. The other is that Christ now stands on that side of reality we call divine. All acknowledge a debt to him as Saviour from sin and death; all see in him God's apostle to men; all worship him as Lord.[5]

III

Finally, we must reckon with Christian testimony down the centuries to the saviourhood of Christ.

What is this testimony worth? Today no argument appeals to men more than 'the argument from experience'. Now in Christianity this means religious experience of Christ, for what nature is to the scientist, Christ is to the Christian believer.

If somebody reminds us that such experience, being subjective, can be delusive, we may heed his warning. But does this mean that all Christian experience of Christ must therefore be discounted? On the contrary, to those who so discount it, the Christian has the right to protest: 'Am I really precluded from all appeal to my personal experience of Christ? Did not the apostles appeal to theirs? Is my experience of Christ as a living Saviour:

> I see thee not, I hear thee not,
> Yet art thou oft with me

quite worthless in settling the objective worth of his person?'

To this some may object, 'If you claim to commune with Christ, you have no right to gird at those who claim to commune with saints or the Blessed Virgin Mary. What difference is there between their experience and yours?'

To this objection there is a two-fold answer. First, in *personal* terms: 'If we are not to doubt absolutely everything, we must find our certainty in what founds and sustains our moral life, and who is this but the living Christ who is 'the same yesterday today and for ever' (*Hebrews* 13:8)? Moreover, if we allow him to have his way with us, the result is not a fleeting experience but a real life-change.'

Second, in *historical* terms: 'Between experience of Christ and experience of a saint there is all the difference in the world. Our Lord has entered history, and abides in it, with such a piercing moral effect, as no saint has ever done. Nor is this all. He has entered the life of the whole Church no less than that of individuals.'

So, to the objector's question, 'Can individual experience of Christ mediate absolute truth?', the answer is two-fold. (1) Our own experience of the living Christ is not a passing impression but is, as it was for the apostles, a life-faith. What does Paul say? 'The *life* that I now live in the flesh, I live by faith' (*Galatians* 2:20). And so have said a countless multitude down the centuries, unknown to fame or the history books. (2) Standing over our own individual experience, and confirming it, is the experience of the world-wide Church for nearly two thousand years.

IV

Towards a Doctrine. Such is the evidence. Let us now seek a solution to the problem of Christ's person.

For Christian thinkers down the years the problem has ever been how to relate the human to the divine, the divine to the human. Thus, at the Council of Chalcedon in 451 AD, the Church's theologians rightly maintained that Christ was truly God and truly man. But their theory of two natures, one human and one divine, united in Christ's person, did not even then win universal approval. Today it no longer appeals. For the truth for which they stood was expressed in a now outmoded philosophy of 'substance'. Nowadays we employ moral and personal categories. What happens when we do so? Apparently our choice lies between two theories of Christ's person: progressive incarnation, i.e. God becoming man, and progressive deification, man becoming God. The first works with the idea of Christ's self-limitation—his *kenōsis*; the second with the idea of Christ's self-fulfilment—his *plerōsis*. But must we choose between them? On the contrary, may we not hope to get nearer the truth about Christ if we *combine* them?

Consider the idea of *kenōsis*, or self-limitation. The apostolic writers, from Paul to John the seer of Patmos, agree that Christ's story did not begin in a Bethlehem cradle but had a prologue in eternity. Thus they speak of his pre-existence.

In the gospels this belief finds support in what has been called 'the Divine Consciousness of Jesus',[6] i.e. his awareness of a unique filial relationship to his heavenly Father. This shines out at the supreme hours of revelation in Jesus' earthly life, notably at his Baptism and on the Mount of Transfiguration. In these sublime crises of his spiritual life Jesus knew himself to be what he really was, and this knowledge was confirmed by constant communion with his heavenly Father. One thinks of hours like that recorded by Luke when 'He rejoiced in the Holy Spirit' and uttered his great thanksgiving (*Luke* 10:21f). In John's gospel this becomes specially clear, as witness Christ's words in the great intercessory prayer, 'Father, glorify me in thy own presence with the glory, which I had with thee before the world was.' (*John* 17:5).

What John here represents Christ as saying was also the belief of the early Christians, as witness the pre-Pauline hymn of the Church quoted by Paul in writing to the Philippians:

> Though in God's form he was ...
> He emptied himself
> Taking a servant's form
> (*Philippians* 2:6f).

More, down the centuries, it has ever been demanded by the adoring faith of the Church, as in the supreme Christian hymn we know as the *Te Deum*:

> Thou art the King of glory, O Christ,
> Thou art the everlasting Son of the Father.

If then there was an eternal prologue to Christ's story, for our Lord there must have been also a great renunciation 'outside the walls of the world'. Before the Son of God entered it, his sacrifice had begun. In becoming man, he must have limited himself, somehow 'laid his glory by'.

But does not this doctrine of *kenōsis* derogate from Christ's divinity? No, God is God when he stoops no less than when he reigns. In becoming man, the Son of God renounced the exercise of divine powers, so that on earth he might live within the limits appointed for mortal men. If somebody objects that this view conflicts with the immutability of God, the answer is that an infinite being who could not reduce himself to this finite world would, by his very inability, be reduced to finitude. If anybody demurs that this doctrine involves cosmic chaos ('What was happening to the rest of the universe when Christ the creative Word was self-emptied?'), the answer is that the New Testament does not teach that the universe was made *by* the Son.[7] Criticise the doctrine of *kenōsis* as we will, we seem unable to dispense with it. Show it the back door, and it will return through the window.

What is its advantage? It gives us a doctrine of Christ's person untroubled by the limitations and ignorances of the incarnate Christ. He consented not to know with a nescience divinely wise; by an act of love's omnipotence he set aside the style of a God and took a servant's form.

The *dis*advantage of the doctrine is that we are left with 'a humbled God' when we need also a royal and redeeming one. Therefore hand in hand with the idea of *kenōsis* or self-limitation, must go that of *plerōsis*, or self-fulfilment.[8]

Think of it this way. Religious experience is made up of two personal and vertical movements: God of his grace seeking man, and man in his turn responding to the divine initiative. Now apply these two movements to Christ. Think of his person not in terms of two natures but as a union of these two personal movements: perfect revelation and perfect religion. In Christ the two were united, involuted. As his personal history ripened by every earthly experience, and he was found equal to every crisis, ever mightier grew the latent Godhead in his life's interior; the more he sacrificially laid down his life for others, the more he gained his own soul.

It was this which the writer to the Hebrews had in mind
(though he talks of 'perfecting' rather than of 'fulfilment')
when he said, 'Son though he was, he learned obedience in
the school of suffering and, once perfected, became the
source of eternal salvation for all who obey him' (*Hebrews*
5:8f, *NEB*). Consider the point made here. For anyone
who has a sense of vocation, as above all others Christ
had, there must be moral growth and ripening. God's Son
though he was, it was not different with Christ. He had to
work himself into his place in God's saving plan by going
down amongst, and suffering with, his brethren whom he
would 'lead to glory'. This was his 'perfecting' or 'self-
fulfilment'; and so, by offering to God a perfect self-
sacrifice (*Hebrews* 10:14), he became a Saviour for all
who put their trust in him. Thus he worked out the salvation which he was, and his life culminated in the perfection
of his own soul and of our salvation in the cross, the
resurrection and the glory.

Christ's life is therefore the story of his recovery by
moral conquest of that mode of being from which, by a
tremendous moral act, he came. Such a view of Christ's
person does justice to the moral side of his human life.
Though his relation to his heavenly Father was immediate
and unbroken, he had no immunity from the moral law
that we must *earn* our greatest legacies and by labour and
suffering appropriate our best gifts.

One important word of postscript. 'You must believe',
said St Augustine, 'if you would understand.' In other
words, to know a person fully, you must 'first love him,
ere to you he will seem worthy of your love.' Down the
centuries worship and adoration no less than thinking and
theorising have enabled Christians to discover 'the truth
as it is in Jesus.' Accordingly, if what the New Testament
and the creeds say about Christ is to be accepted, there

must be a personal response to the challenge with which God confronts us in his Son.

To the natural man, in the pride of his intellect, this sounds absurd. He supposes the mystery of Christ's person is to be solved intellectually, without any idea of self-commitment to him. Experience proves him mistaken. Take the natural man's approach, and Christ will remain for you an enigma. Only faith and love know who Christ really is; and Christian faith is the decision to commit our whole soul and future to the confidence that Christ is not an illusion but the reality of God.

'He comes to us as One unknown', wrote Albert Schweitzer, 'as of old, by the lakeside; he came to those who knew him not. He speaks to us the same word: "Follow thou me!" and sets us to the tasks which he has to fulfil for our time. He commands. And to those who obey him, whether they be wise or simple, he will reveal himself in the toils, the conflicts and the sufferings which they will pass through in his fellowship, and, as an ineffable mystery, they shall learn in their own experience who he is.'[9]

NOTES

1. C. W. F. Smith, *The Jesus of the Parables*, pp 287f.

2. The seven 'I am' sayings, parables of his person, in John's gospel expand, theologically, the claims made by Jesus in the first three. The synoptic 'points' become 'stars' in the Fourth Gospel.

3. See the author's *Gospel and Apostle*, chapter 11, for a defence of their authenticity.

4. This chapter, and especially its closing verses, may be called the *locus classicus* for apostolic inspiration.

5. In the Greek Old Testament (the Bible of the early Christians) *Kyrios*, 'Lord', renders the Hebrew word for Jehovah (*Adonai*), i.e. it was a divine title. So, in the Dead Sea Scrolls *Mar* (or *Mare*) is a name for God. See F. F. Bruce, *Paul, Apostle of the Free Spirit*, p 117.

6. See V. Taylor, *The Person of Christ*, pp 155-189.
7. V. Taylor, *The Person of Christ*, p 267.
8. So P. T. Forsyth in his *magnum opus*: *The Person and Place of Jesus Christ*.
9. *The Quest of the Historical Jesus*, p 401. These oft-quoted words with which Schweitzer closed his book are hard to square with the picture of Christ as a deluded apocalyptist which he had painted earlier in it (p 369). For how could this 'immeasurably great man' whose career ended so tragically and finally on the cross (there is not a word about his resurrection), still 'come to us today' and set us to the tasks he wants us to fulfil?

His own later heroic work as a missionary in the swamps of Lambarene suggests that the last words of his book more truly reflect his view about Christ implying, as they do, not an apocalyptist who was 'destroyed' at Calvary, but One who still lives and challenges us to follow him. Such was the 'mysticism' not of Paul but of Albert Schweitzer!

Epilogue

Our study has been mainly of Christ and the kingdom and their first interpreters in the gospels and epistles. But the process of interpretation did not end with the New Testament, nor could it as the gospel moved out more and more into the Gentile world which thought in Greek and not Hebrew terms. So in the early Christian centuries we see it in process of being thus redefined, as at the Council of Chalcedon in AD 451.

Re-definition is difficult and can be dangerous, so easy is it to change the gospel into something quite different that an Athanasius has to decline all compromise with an Arius if the truth about Christ is to be safeguarded. Moreover, old titles of majesty need to be replaced by new ones. The Lord Jesus becomes God the Son; the Holy Spirit God the Holy Ghost, and the doctrine of the Trinity, present germinally in the New Testament, comes to be explicitly formulated.

The Reformation brings with it not only the removal of dubious accretions to the faith but the re-discovery of New Testament truths in peril of eclipse. Thus Luther recovers the doctrine of justification by God's grace through faith (which, though Pauline, has its roots deep in Christ's teaching) when it is in danger of submersion beneath a theology of 'merit', and in his hands

> The thing becomes a trumpet
> Whence he blows soul-animating strains.

Still today the process of interpretation goes on, as it always must as men's thought-world changes, if Christ and the gospel are to come livingly home to men in their day.

In our time perhaps boldest of all was Bultmann's proposal to re-interpret the 'myths' of the New Testament in terms of his friend Heidegger's existential philosophy. The New Testament 'myths'—a three-storeyed universe, angels and demons at war, nature-miracles, and a pre-existent Christ who comes down from heaven to redeem men—are, said Bultmann, first-century ways of describing human existence and Christian salvation, and may still be made relevant to science-minded modern man if he will but re-interpret them in existential ways. Here is a modern philosophical cradle in which the gospel can be laid, without adulterating its essential message, and with the hope of making it speak to man's predicament today.

But was this existentialism the kindly cradle which Bultmann supposed it to be? 'Heidegger—Cuckoo or Cradle?' asked David Cairns in his book *Gospel without Myth?*, and answered his question by pronouncing it a cuckoo which, unless summarily dealt with, would shoulder the Christian chicks from the nest. *Non tali auxilio!* If Bultmann's proposal to give us 'Christianity without tears' were adopted, we might end up in 'tears without Christianity'.

It is time to draw our discussion of Christ and the kingdom to a close.

Where stands 'the household of faith' today? Now, as in the days of the apostles, the Church lives 'between the times', between D-Day and V-Day when, as we believe, the full meaning of what God did for sinners in Christ will be disclosed and (as somebody has picturesquely put it) the world will end not 'with a bang or a whimper', but with the sound of a trumpet and 'all heaven will be let loose.'

Of this blessed consummation we may speak only in

symbol and in 'myth', though for us Christians 'myth', so far from meaning a fairy-tale or a discredited first-century thought-form, is

> . . . the language which contains the clue
> To that which is at once both real and true.

And here John the Seer of Patmos, whom space has not allowed us to quote much in these pages, may be permitted the last words:

> I saw a new heaven and a new earth
> (*Revelation* 21:1).

> They shall hunger no more, neither thirst any more: the sun shall not strike them, nor any scorching heat. For the Lamb in the midst of the throne will be their shepherd, and he will guide them to springs of living water; and God will wipe away every tear from their eyes. (*Revelation* 7:16f).

> And they shall reign for ever and ever
> (*Revelation* 22:5).

Then the new face which God put on human life when he gave his only Son for us men and for our salvation will no longer need interpreting. For if now, like Paul, 'we see through a mirror, dimly', then it will be 'face to face'.

Some Technical Terms

Like the scientist or the physician, the theologian has his own stock-in-trade of technical terms. Here are a dozen of the commonest ones.

Anthropomorphism: The attribution to God of human characteristics.

Atonement: 'At-one-ment'. The reconciliation of God and man through the 'work' of Christ.

Beatitude: heavenly happiness, but applied also to Christ's 'blessed sayings' (*Matthew* 5:3-12).

Christology: the doctrine of Christ's nature and person.

Ecclesiology: the doctrine of the Church (Greek: *ecclesia*), or people of God.

Eschatology: from the Greek adjective *eschatos* (last). The doctrine of the end (*eschaton*), or 'last things' (*eschata*); namely, judgment, heaven and hell.

Eucharist: Greek, *eucharistia* (thanksgiving): the Lord's Supper, or Holy Communion.

Incarnation: from the Latin *in* plus *caro* (flesh). The doctrine that the eternal Son of God took human flesh. See *John* 1:14.

Kenōsis: Greek, 'emptying' (see *Philippians* 2:8, '*heauton ekenson*', 'he emptied himself '). The doctrine of the self-limitation of Christ in becoming man.

Parousia: Greek, 'presence' or 'arrival'. In the New Testament Christ's future coming in glory.

Q: usually, from German *Quelle* meaning 'source'. The scholars' shorthand description for the collection of Jesus' sayings used by both *Matthew* and *Luke*.

Synoptic: adjective derived from the Greek noun *synopsis* (seeing together), and applied to the first three gospels

because they present a common outline of Jesus' ministry.
Theodicy: from the Greek *theos* (God) and *diké* (justice).
The vindication of the ways of God with men. See, for
example, P. T. Forsyth's *The Justification of God* (1917).